Black Dawn, Bright Day

Indian Prophecies for the Millennium
That Reveal the Fate of the Earth

Sun Bear with Wabun Wind

A FIRESIDE BOOK
Published by Simon & Schuster
New York   London   Toronto   Sydney   Tokyo   Singapore

 FIRESIDE
Simon & Schuster Building
Rockefeller Center
1230 Avenue of the Americas
New York, New York 10020

First Fireside Edition, 1992

FIRESIDE and colophon are registered
trademarks of Simon & Schuster, Inc.

Manufactured in the United States of America

10

Library of Congress Cataloging-in-Publication Data

Sun Bear (Chippewa Indian)
    Black dawn, bright day : Indian prophecies for the
millennium that reveal the fate of the earth's environment /
Sun Bear, Wabun Wind.
        p.   cm.
    ISBN 0-671-75900-0
    "A Sun Bear book."
    1. Prophecies (Occultism)   2. Human ecology—Miscellanea.
I. Wind, Wabun, 1945-   II. Title.
BF1791.S86   1992
133.3—dc20
                                                    91-27128
                                                         CIP

Dedication

This book is dedicated to the Great Spirit and the Earth Mother, to all the people of the Bear Tribe Medicine Society who labor on behalf of my vision, and, with special thanks and love, to Jaya Bear.

Acknowledgements

I want to thank the many people all around the world who have supplied me with information for this book. I particularly acknowledge my Spirit sources who have given me the visions and have helped me find the pattern in the past that shows the future.

Special thanks to Matt Ryan, who gathered a lot of the Earth changes information for me, both in his capacity as editor of *Wildfire* magazine and out of his own deep interest in the Earth. Thanks to Dr. James DeMeo, and his excellent publication, *Pulse Of The Planet*. I also want to give a general thanks to all my apprentices, students, and friends who sent in information.

A number of people helped Wabun and me with various stages of preparing this book. With Dawn Songfeather Davies' competent help we were able to complete the manuscript much more quickly than our schedules would have otherwise allowed. Thanks to Kim Lawrence, Chuck Engler and Jim Gavitt for help with early typing and corrections.

Rick Yandrick of Eastern Informational Systems in Doylestown, Pennslyvania, began the work on the Earth changes maps. George Monacelli of Bear Tribe Publishing expanded and completed the maps that appear in Chapter Twelve. Many thanks to them. Thanks to our editors at Goldmann Verlag in Germany for originally contacting us about this book, and for helping it transform from *I Believe* to *Black Dawn/Bright Day*. Thanks to Jerry Chasen for helping with the contract work. And special thanks to Sherry Lancaster, Christine Alexanian and Matt Ryan in their capacity as editors at Bear Tribe Publishing.

Thanks to Kim Lawrence and George Monacelli for the design of the book, and to Scott Guynup for the beautiful cover art and design.

Wabun thanks the people who helped her work on this book while she was in Peru, and gives special thanks to Thomas and Kyla Wind for their love and support.

Contents

Part I — *Black Dawn*

Part II — *Bright Day*

Black Dawn

Chapter One

The Natural World

To understand the nature of the things that are happening now upon the Earth Mother, we first have to understand different concepts of relating to the Earth. The Native people of Turtle Island, the North American Indians, relate to the Earth as the mother of all living creation. Native people also believe all creatures — minerals, plants, animals, spirits — have the same right to life as humans do.

Native people try to blend with nature, rather than conquer it. The Native philosophy teaches that you never take anything from the Earth without first making your prayers. Before you go out on a hunt you always make prayers and ceremonies of thanksgiving. Before you take the life of an animal you say, "I have to take your life, little brother, little sister, so that I may continue my own. Even as I take your life this time, the time will come when I will give my life back to the Earth. I too will become part of the cycle of life. My body will give new life for the plants, animals and insects to feed on. From my sacred sacrifice a new life will come up again."

Whenever we take a plant, we never take the first one we come to. We regard that one as a grandfather plant. We make an offering there. We say, "Grandfather, we come to your plant people in order to have food or to have medicine for our healing. We make a gift to you and we pray that your species will always be on the Earth." Then we take from the other plants of that species nearby the grandfather. But we take only what we need.

This is our sacred way. It insures there will always be plenty of every thing for generations to come. It is a Native philosophy found across the Earth that *you never kill anything you don't eat; you don't waste anything.* This is part of our religion, part of living in balance and harmony upon the Earth.

This is what the ghostdancers sing in their dance songs — all giving, all receiving, all part of the sacred way. And the healing of the Earth happens in this way. If you watch nature, you see how each part of creation feeds on the other. When the leaves go back to the soil, they provide food for the Earth and for the other plants that are there. The rabbits eat from the grasses and the plants, and in turn, some of the larger four-leggeds come and eat the rabbits. It's all a covenant, an agreement among all living things. There's a balance and harmony this way.

For thousands of years, Native people have said, "This is our Earth Mother. You can't take from her all the time, you have to give back to her." You can't just take, take, take. You have to say your prayers and only take what you need. You must keep in harmony and balance with the Earth.

We feel that all living creation around us is intelligent and that every thing has a right to be here as much as people do. We think of the Earth Mother as being an intelligent, living being.

Today, we need to think that way again; we need to learn from the Native traditions. For perhaps as long as twenty thousand years, the Native people lived so harmoniously on Turtle Island that the first Europeans who arrived here were able to describe it as a beautiful, unspoiled wilderness, a virtual paradise. But in the short period of four hundred and fifty years since the Europeans arrived, this continent has become riddled with ecological disasters and pollution from sea to shining sea. Look hard at what has happened in that very short time span, then ask yourself "Why?"

When the Europeans first came to this land, we Natives went out and showed them how to plant crops. We would plant corn, beans and squash and put the remains of a fish in the dirt with the seeds. We kept telling the Europeans, "You have to feed the Earth." But they said, "Well, that's just a savage custom." They didn't understand what we were saying.

It wasn't until the New England States had eroded away that the Europeans became even a little bit aware of what we had been trying to tell them. Yet when the great Dust

Bowl of the 1930's occurred, the one that wiped out thousands of acres of land, the dominant society still called the Indians the savages. But we Indians disagreed. We called those who had destroyed the land the "wheat savages" because, year after year, they had planted wheat until they had destroyed the Earth in certain areas to the point where the land wasn't capable of producing anything.

The same pattern has gone on and on. We have to learn to love and respect the Earth as a living being in the sacred manner now!

"Indian Givers"

Different concepts about land caused conflict between the Native people and the European people. The Native people accepted the Europeans at first and treated them royally. The Native philosophy is that you treat the stranger as the Great Spirit in disguise. This is the standard way of hospitality which is sacred to the Native people. When they sat down with the European strangers, they would bring gifts. When they offered these gifts, the people from across the Great Water said, "Oh, these primitive savages, they think we're gods." Their arrogance got away with them because they didn't understand the sacred ways.

The root of the problem is a different way of thinking. It is a basic difference in life philosophy that has brought about all this destruction. When the Europeans came to Turtle Island, they looked at it as land that was there for the taking. They had to kill a few Indians to get it, but history shows that was no problem for them.

At the time the first Europeans came to the continental United States, there were at least three million Native people living here. By the time that the Europeans had finished their slaughter in 1900, there were only 300,000 Natives left. Since then we've regenerated. There are about 1,400,000 Native people in the United States at this time.

At first, however, the Europeans — few in number — asked the Native people if they would share with them.

4

They asked the Indians if they would give them a little land. The Native people had a great sense of generosity. They said, "Well yes, you are our brothers. You share the same mother with us, so here is some land for you." After a while the Europeans weren't happy with that. They kept saying to the Natives, "Move over a little, we need more land." Then the immigrants over-strained the Indians' generosity and started forcibly driving the Indians out of their homelands. They began to take more and more land, often at the point of a gun.

The Natives couldn't understand the concept of the settlers owning the land. They thought the Europeans were using the land as they did. That meant that other people also had the right to go there. Pretty soon there were conflicts because of these different concepts, and the Europeans began killing Native people. To avoid conflict many Natives simply retreated to more remote areas, hoping to avoid the new settlers.

Originally the Native chiefs had brought gifts to honor the European men. They asked for their gifts back after they saw the killing that was happening. "You haven't honored the gift," they said. "You haven't shown friendship." This is where the expression "Indian-giver" comes from. It was the Indian answer to the European practice of not keeping a treaty or agreement. To the Indian people this showed that the gift of friendship or land had no value to the recipient anymore.

Every bit of the land is sacred to the Native people. When the European settlers came across this land, they didn't understand this sacredness. They didn't respect the land, so the Natives resisted them. I have read that it cost the government eight federal soldiers for every Indian they killed. The Spaniards eventually called the Indians the bronze race that knew how to die, because many Indians preferred dying to yielding.

As the Europeans moved across the American continent, history shows that the average man, in his lifetime, used up three farms. He would cut down the timber and leave it lying on the Earth, or set fires and burn beautiful virgin forest so he could have land to plant crops. This is what happened in the New England States. You can still see old stone fences going up through brush and small timber in places there. These stone fences marked the boundaries of the farms that were used and then abandoned.

These people just wore out the soil. They never bothered to take care of it or to use proper crop practices. As a result, they had to keep moving westward in order to have productive farmland. And as they went, they continued to cut down trees and kill Indians. Almost all of the beautiful forests that had been here for thousands of years were destroyed at that time. Massive deforestation and genocide were part of the famous, "glorious" movement westward.

When the settlers reached the Great Plains, they discovered the buffalo and stopped farming for a time. In a period of about forty years these "American Heroes" slaughtered 50 million or more buffalo. Think of it. They killed at least *50,000,000 buffalo.* Why? Because it was easier and more profitable than farming. They killed them primarily for just their hides and tongues, both of which were highly valued in the East and in Europe.

During the time that the railroads were being built, people would ride on the railroad and shoot buffalo for sport. They would often kill up to a thousand buffalo on one of these sporting expeditions. They used these beautiful animals for target practice. They shot them and just let the meat and hides lay and rot.

The immigrants who came to the Northwest didn't even bother to cut down the trees to prepare land for farming; they just bored holes in the bottom of beautiful pines and firs, some of which were 125 feet tall. The sap, which is the life-blood of these trees, flowed down into these holes. Then these "Conquering Heroes" would set fire to them. The trees became living torches, dying from their own burning

6

pitch.

In this way the settlers burned down thousands of acres of forests just so they could farm the land. These European immigrants destroyed beautiful trees without any concern for what was happening. They would also cut the trees off the tops of the mountains and never bother to replant them. Even today, when you fly over the western part of the United States, you see whole mountaintops that look bare of trees. They've been clear-cut and replaced with seedlings that will take a century to become a forest again.

By the time the European immigrants got to the west coast of the United States, they had "refined" not only their treatment of the trees, but also of the Indians. They didn't just go and shoot Indians on sight, like they had done in the East. Instead, they would invite them to a feast. They'd say, "Well come on and have a big feast with us." And then they would poison the food. The Indians would eat it, fall ill and die. If any tried to escape, their "hosts" would slaughter them. That was one way they solved the "Indian problem."

All of these practices show the ways in which the European immigrants dealt with the land, the animals and the people. They were all part of the movement westward across America, even though these stories have been omitted in the famous, romanticized versions recorded in the history books.

All Of Creation

Before we Native American people look at adding anything to our life, we pray over it. We ask, "How does this affect our life? How does it affect all the rest of creation upon the Earth? How does it affect our relationship to our Creator, and all the generations to come?" That's what we ask ourselves before we bring something new into our life path. We know that we are not here just for ourselves. We're responsible for everything on the planet, everything that we come into contact with. That has to be acknowledged. In our life, when we're just little children, that's put into our minds.

When we go into the sweat lodge, we're reminded of that. We say, "All my relations" or "Thank you, all my relations." By this we mean all other parts of creation on the Earth; all things are our relatives. We are acknowledging them. When we fill the pipe, we also acknowledge all of creation because we know everything has to live the same as we do. That's what we Natives have come to, this sense of interconnection. That is what we strive to always be aware of. Many humans are not willing to wake up to this interconnection and the responsibility that comes with it. We Native teachers try to reach out to those humans who are ready to listen. That's our responsibility. It can get kind of lonely. That's why I'd like to have many more people on the planet aware of what is happening. I'm trying to bring you a message and an understanding so you'll know both how to wake up and how to stay alive.

I'm a Native American talking to you through the pages of this book. But I drink the same water and breathe the same air as you do, so I am truly your brother. We all share many of the same things. Nobody can get away from the condition the Earth is in now. Nobody can say, "Hey, I can get away from it." We have to look at the planetary condition. That's why I'm sharing with people. I have to get your attention. We all need to become more aware and to understand why the Earth changes are occurring.

To understand the reality of what is happening, we have to look at the contrast of the two different ideologies that move through the world. One is the Native philosophy, the sacred way of walking on the planet by blending with nature and being part of nature. The other ideology demands conquest of nature.

The people who came from across the Great Water had what I call the "ladder" approach. The ladder approach has God at the top, then man, then woman, and then the kids, then the cat and dog, then the rest of the creation according to how useful it is to man. The European concept was that they had the supreme right to do anything they wanted to with anything under them on this ladder. They had no sense of respect, no sense of the totality of things.

In the Native philosophy, we think of life as a circle. All things are part of the circle. All parts of the creation have the same right to life as we do. The animal, the plant, the mineral, the elemental kingdoms — all creation belongs to that circle. Nothing is above and nothing is below. We think of things in terms of roundness. All things have a roundness to them: the Earth, the Sun, the Moon, the stars. The trees and rocks have roundness, and humans have roundness as well. The lodges we build — our sweatlodge, our tepee — are also round because we want to acknowledge the wholeness of creation.

Sharp Edges

Then the Europeans came along and built square things. Squareness has a hardness to it — it's those sharp edges coming out all the time. Squareness was also a way that people thought. As the Europeans cut the land up into squares so that everybody had their own little block, they even began to think in terms of squareness.

People in such societies have come to think that's the way it should be. Their thinking reflects these sharp edges, and their sense of territory. In these societies people talk about "my house, my car, my wife, my dog, my land." There is no longer the sense of oneness with all of creation. The value of land is measured only by how much it is worth to someone else in terms of dollars. This is a totally different way of looking at things.

When we look at these ideas, we see how they have created what we have today. They separated us from each other, blocked us off from one another so completely we can no longer reach out and embrace as brothers and sisters. We no longer have a sense of responsibility for one another; we lost that with the ladder view of life.

We need to consider here what we have done to each other and, consequently, what we have done to the planet, since the two are deeply connected. We need to look at the beginnings of how we relate. In doing so, I will push some people's buttons because some of you have some little left-over concepts from your conditioning that might bother you as we explore this area.

Sacred Circles

At one time, all people upon the Earth worshipped in a sacred manner. They acknowledged the forces and the powers of creation all around them. All over the world, they worshipped in sacred ceremonial circles. In the United States there were some 20,000 medicine wheels, sacred circles where people would come to do their ceremonies and their praying and to seek and share knowledge with each other. A medicine man or medicine woman would come to such a circle, empty out their medicine pouch and say, "We can use this particular herb for healing this, and use this one for healing that." This was one way the knowledge was shared at the sacred circle.

We find sacred circles in Europe too. Along with Stonehenge, great stone circles can be found all over England. In Germany I saw a stone circle and a turtle's head was marked on one of the stones, and I said, "Oh yes, I know you folks, I recognize all this." I saw pictographs there of the bear shaman and the deer shaman — ancient acknowledgements of these forces. The cave writings there are also from Native Europeans who, like the Native Americans, worked in a sacred manner with the Earth and with all things.

Then something happened that is crucial to understanding what is transpiring in the world today. About 5,000 years ago a religion began that wouldn't tolerate other religions. The people starting this religion said, "This is the only way that things can be done." And then they began to watch the people. Any time they saw that people were going to squirm out from under their control, they would add another little law, another rule. In this way their religion constructed a very dogmatic approach to thinking.

The proponents of this new religion eventually murdered nine million people in Europe who were practicing the old religions of the Earth and using the sacred circle. In the old ways, somebody could go out and build a circle of stones in two or three hours, do their ceremonies and offer their prayers. There was no need to build any big cathedrals. In fact, there was no way you could get people following this path to build a place where the priests would take over religion for everyone and start collecting money for their "service."

The proponents of the new religion put many labels on those people who used the sacred ways. They said they were "bad people" because they weren't worshipping God as the new religious folks defined *Him*. They called those who followed the old ways "pagans," which literally means "countryman." They said, "Well, these are a bunch of country bumpkins. They don't worship the way we do."

The oppressors of the Earth religions started to get worried about things they couldn't understand or control, including the powerful life energy that would come through the people who worshipped the Sacred Mother. The Earth worshippers didn't need priests; they could pray, do a chant, and bring in the rain, the thunderbeings and the other forces. They could also use their life energy to heal.

The new philosophers — Christians and others — saw these powers. That was when they got worried about being able to control the people who practiced the old ways. They said, "These people here can set up things themselves. We aren't able to control them. We've got to get control over them for our philosophy to win. If we can't control them, we must kill them." So they wiped out nine million people. They had to kill them to take power over the other people in Europe. Once they had this power, they tried to neuter their followers by making them forget the life force that flowed through them.

The Native people of Europe, as well as America, knew of the natural force, the life force. They worked with it as the primary force within each one of us and within all the rest of creation. One manifestation of the life force that we feel is sexual energy.

The people's understanding of the life force worried the new philosophers because it was something that was in all the creation; they couldn't get a monopoly on it. The Natives knew how to call on and work with the life force. So the leaders of the new religion said, "Well, we're going to have to put this energy into a little box and put it up on the shelf. It's going to have to be a 'No-No,' a 'Thou Shalt Not.'"

The repression of people's life force was also aided by bringing little bits and pieces of things from the former traditions into the new religion. They were used if it seemed like they would do some good in convincing people to adopt the new religion. For instance, the Greeks had a myth about a fiery place where an underworld god tortured people. "Hey, that looks pretty good," the new philosophers said. "That might keep some of these people straight." So they put it in their doctrine and said, "If you get out of line, not only are you going to get punished by the priest and hung on the rack now, but afterwards we're going to twist you on this little spit and roast you for the next 10,000 years or longer."

That idea seemed to scare the people who used to follow the natural ways. So the new philosophers figured they would make it part of their doctrine. It helped them see how they could control people through fear. Shortly after they got power, these new philosophers — a repressed bunch of fanatics — went to work on the sexual ideas people had.

At first the leaders of the new religion weren't concerned about marriage, but then they realized they needed to get more control over people's sexuality. That was an area where the expression of life force was taking power away from them. Sexually fulfilled people aren't as impressed by authority as sexually frustrated ones are. The new religious authorities wanted to control every bit of a person's life, from the cradle to the grave. So they instituted monogamous marriage, and included everything else having to do with sex among their "Thou Shalt Nots."

Here and there, little pockets of people hid up in the hills and the wilderness and kept to the old ways. The word wilderness itself means, "wild land beyond control of man." And that's where the people of the Earth religions had to go: back with their brothers — the bears, the wolves, and the foxes — if they were going to survive. The old teachers who survived hid out and quietly kept their sacred teachings alive.

These old teachers had great knowledge and great power, but they were almost destroyed by the new philosophers. This near-destruction of a way of life became part of the whole circle, the long-range process that has brought us to this time of cleansing.

After the new Christian philosophers "fixed up" things in Europe to suit their philosophy, they discovered there were other places to go. They headed out for these "new lands."

Getting The Gold

The Spaniards were the first ones to reach the new lands and get entrenched. They came looking for gold and discovered vast amounts of it in South America and Mexico. All they had to do to get it was murder all the leaders of the Central and South American Natives. They did this with no problem. In doing so, many of the sacred teachers were murdered also.

The Spaniards saw the universities and libraries with volumes and volumes of teachings. But the Spaniards weren't interested in Native knowledge. All these "civilized" men wanted was gold. They forced the Natives into slave labor to mine the gold, build their homes, grow their food and provide for their other needs. Then the Catholic Church in the form of the padres came along to "save heathen souls." The only dispute between the missionaries and the conquistadors was over who was going to get the Indian slaves, and who would get the most out of the land they conquered. Both the priests and the conquistadors tortured the Natives in all kinds of hideous ways, then took from them everything they could.

Before long, England, France and the other "civilized" countries found out that the Spaniards were getting all the gold. They each decided to get some of it for themselves. So they set up a bunch of thieves to attack Spanish ships. They called these thieves pirates. They became so popular the government even knighted them. Sir Francis Drake and Sir Walter Raleigh were both pirates. At that time in England, if someone was able to bring in a shipload of gold, he could have just about any title he wanted. The pirate Henry Morgan became a government official. These people received gifts and titles for slitting Spanish throats.

The Spanish ships would have 30 or 40 guns; then the English would come in with a 50-gun ship. Next the Spanish ships would go up to 80 guns. The ships' firepower kept increasing until there were as many as 120 to 150 guns on a ship. Then the ships started sailing in armadas to protect the gold. The Spaniards would send out 20 or 30 warships at a time to protect their gold ships.

The English, the Dutch, the French and other Europeans all stole from the Spaniards. But when the sea battles became too dangerous, the other European countries said, "Let's go find some Indians of our own that we can steal from." So they went and formed colonies in North America.

Shortly after Captain John Smith and the rest of the first colonists arrived from England, the colonists were about ready to whack Smith's head off because he couldn't find any Indians with gold to steal from. The Indians he found had only corn. The colonists weren't happy with that. Corn wasn't really what they wanted.

Their original intention for coming to the New World was for everybody to get wealthy by stealing from the Indians, and then go back to the old country and become gentlemen there. That was the purpose of the trading companies too, like the Hudson Bay Company — which is still operating. Go to the new land and steal everything possible from the Indians.

At first, the Indians tried to help the colonists in a respectful manner. But sometimes, in the middle of the winter, the settlers would run out of corn because they had been too lazy to get their act together and raise their own. So the settlers would raid the Indian villages, threaten the people's lives, and kill a few to force those remaining into giving them corn and other food. That was the way the Europeans treated their "new brothers." That was also when the Indian people began to resist. The Indian wars were a result of this duplicity.

I always have to smile a little bit when I start hearing people tell about their ancestors who came over on the Mayflower or when I hear about the Daughters of the American Revolution. I smile because it doesn't take too much research to find out that a lot of the early colonists had a choice between coming here or staying in a European debtors' prison.

One of the ways the authorities got women to come to America was to find old Sadie out on the street peddling something she could only peddle in London and say, "Well, lady, would you like to spend five years in jail, or would you like to go to the new land and be a bride for one of our fine, brave men over there?" In that way they rounded up about 200 streetwalkers in London and sent them to the colonies to be brides. So debtors and prostitutes were among the "good" people, those staunch citizens who first landed on this continent.

The other "good" people were religious folk who held particular beliefs that didn't fit within the Catholic Church or the Church of England. These people left Europe because they had been persecuted for their religious beliefs. However, when they got to the New World, they turned out to be bigoted bastards too, just like the people they had left behind.

These good people used all kinds of little treatments on other people who didn't do things exactly their way. For example, they devised a seat on a pole where they'd sit offenders and drop them in the water, and if they didn't repent from their evil ways, they'd drop them in again. In Massachusetts and other places, they'd whip people clean across the state line. They even whipped people from some of the more recognized religions, like the Quakers, because they didn't share the religion which predominated at a particular place and time.

Needless to say, few of these advocates of "religious freedom" wanted to extend that freedom to the Native people who were already living here. For example, there was a "gentleman" named Cotton Mather whose approach to things was that any person who didn't practice religion his way, and who didn't believe in God exactly as he did, was going to hell. And he devoted himself to putting them there. At one point, Cotton Mather and a troop of his good Christian brothers surrounded a village of peaceful Indians and set fire to the stockade and the village houses. They shot and killed every Indian man, woman, and child who tried to escape. In his autobiography, Mather writes, " . . . and thus I sent 400 of the Red Devils to hell today."

After he got done with that, Mather moved on to other exciting pursuits. In Salem, Massachusetts, he started helping with the practice of witch burnings, which had been brought here from the old country. Several women were burned as witches. Others were tortured and killed in different ways. The people who did these things claimed to be doing "God's work."

Remember that. It's very important to remember all the things that have been done in God's name. When the

Germans marched during World War II, "Gott Mit Uns" (God is With Us) was on their belt buckles. Meanwhile, the American chaplains were praying to God for the success of their troops in killing Germans.

And don't forget that nice American Methodist minister from Colorado named Colonel Shivington. He wanted to go Indian-hunting — a popular sport out West in the mid to late 1800's — so he formed the Colorado Volunteers. Anybody who had a gun and was willing to join could be part of his group; he didn't particularly care about their beliefs. The Colorado Volunteers went out and found the village where Black Kettle, a peaceful, old, Cheyenne chief, and his people were camped under a flag of truce. This "gentleman," this bastard, surrounded the village and murdered every Indian in it except for the few who somehow managed to escape. His troops also indulged in a favorite sport at that time: cutting off the breasts of Indian women and making tobacco pouches out of them. Years later, using Jews in place of Indians, Adolf Hitler continued this practice.

This approach to the Native people — the attitude that the only good Indian was a dead Indian — continued in the United States until around 1900. From the 1600's until then, the Indian population dropped from some 3 million people to 300,000. Whole tribes were decimated, completely wiped out.

The settlers employed every possible means to kill Indians. There are even documented cases of the United States government giving out blankets with smallpox germs on them to the Indians. Still, some tribes continued to fight to their last man. To break down the Natives' resistance, the United States government set up reservations on land they thought was the least likely to have any value. The reservations were pieces of God-forsaken land that nobody else wanted. They herded the Indians into these places and kept them there under military control. Then, of course, the government claimed that it was really sad that the Indians

17

didn't have farming skills and couldn't raise food for themselves, even though in reality the ground was a rock pile or a desert.

Swallow A Religion

Whenever the reservations didn't succeed in breaking Native resistance, the government let the "good religious people" have a try. In New York, the Christian denominations set up something called a "mission board." The board's purpose was to divide up the reservations and determine which denomination would get each reservation. Consequently, the Native people of the United States were given neither freedom of religion nor freedom *from* religion. They were told, in effect, that they should open their mouths and swallow whichever religion the mission board gave them — Presbyterian, Methodist or whatever.

If they tried to practice their Native religion — and this is documented in the records of the old Bureau of Indian Affairs — the penalty for the first offense was a month in prison; for the second, three months. After that, they could get up to five years in prison. Many Hopi people were imprisoned for almost their entire life because they refused to send their children to government schools and to accept the white man's religion.

It wasn't until 1978, when the Indian Freedom of Religion Act was passed, that the government gave us Natives some opportunity to practice our own religions without the threat of being put in prison. Yet, even today the state of Oregon arrests Indians for practicing certain of their religious beliefs.

To further discourage the Native religions, the churches set up a practice whereby they issued food and clothing to the "good" Indians, defined as those who attended church. They denied this help to other Natives.

When I lived in Reno, Nevada, I started a Self-Help Project to assist the Indian people in improving their housing. I got paint donated and started painting houses with volunteer labor. One of the clergymen there suggested I should paint the houses of the "good" people first.

"Who are they?" I asked.

"Well, those who go to church," he said.

"No," I told him, "the paint is going to fall on the just and the unjust alike."

I started at the south end of the Indian colony and painted north.

The missions, on the other hand, made sure nothing good fell on the "unjust." Their approach to the Native people on the reservations was not to help them grow and become whole human beings, it was to keep them as semi-slaves. The missions would tell the Natives, "You must submit to this." They took away the Natives' own spirituality which gave them their power. Anything that empowers the individual is contrary to the teachings of religions that want all the power to be with the priests or clergy.

There were a lot of things the colonists didn't understand about the Indian people. Yet their lack of understanding didn't stop them from wanting to destroy the Indian customs and make us submit to theirs.

Some of the clergymen had interesting experiences with the Indians. One of them even wrote that these poor people didn't know sin. He was right. Native people didn't have any concept of sin. And the lack of sin and guilt was really hard for the colonists to handle. As one Indian said, "The white man brought the good book in one hand to save us from the sins he brought in the other."

When the padres voyaged along the coast of California, they saw beautiful Indian women wearing only grass skirts, with their bronze breasts showing. The padres couldn't handle that. It was really hard for them to see such beauty and naturalness, so they said, "This is sinful." But for thousands of years the women had been dressing that way. That was the proper way for them to dress, given their weather and customs. The only place there was sin was in the padres' heads.

The Native people had a very strong, sacred commitment to their spirituality. When the Lewis and Clark Expedition came westward across the lands of the different Indian tribes, they were particularly impressed with the Nez Perce Indians. They said that these people, though they had never read the Bible, followed its commandments and even went beyond them. One man wrote in his diary, "Here are a people — a nation of savages? No, never. Perhaps a nation of Saints." He said this because of the people's kindness and their love of everyone. In all the time that the expedition travelled among the Nez Perce, they never lost anything. When their horses strayed, they were brought back.

This was the way of my people. When asked about the Indians, an old trader who had a trading post up in Montana said, "As long as they wear their hair long, I would give them the whole store and trust them to pay me for it. But when they cut their hair short, then I start watching them because then they are taking on the white man's ways."

Then there's the story of an Indian guide in Minnesota who was traveling in the woods with a white man. Every time the white man got ready to go to sleep at night, he would take his wallet out and put it under his pillow. Finally, the Indian chuckled and said, "Oh, you don't need to worry about it, there's not another white man within fifty miles of here!" My traditional people have a totally different concept of morality. It's something that is hard for the dominant society to understand.

Before the Europeans "resettled" the Native people in the name of sin and salvation, we were the successful caretakers of all the land on this continent. Now less than 50 million acres are under any kind of Native control. And the United States government and various other deceitful people are still trying to rip off what little the Natives have.

In the United States today, there is a 75 percent unemployment rate on many of the Indian reservations. There is a 70 percent alcoholism rate, and there are many totally destitute people who have nothing, not even a way of getting beyond the cycle of poverty and helplessness. And it is sad to see the same things happening also in Mexico, Central and South America. I see Native people in total poverty in all these places. But I feel more sorry for my own Native people in this country than for the people in these other places because many of them are at least able to live from the land. Those who haven't been lured into cities raise their own food and crops.

I also feel a great sadness for the people of Africa. The missionaries bear a very strong responsibility for what happened to the people there, too. When the missionaries moved into Africa and taught the Natives the "good words," they never bothered to support the people's sense that they had the power to do anything for themselves. The missionaries never acknowledged in them any sense that they were decent human beings. They just took their power from them.

This is an indictment against religious people who are still trying to take power away from people. We have to look at what has been done as part of this dance that was permitted in the name of God.

A Step In The Right Direction

In the late 1980's, a council of churches in the Northwest, which included Lutheran, Methodist, Baptist and Roman Catholic, apologized to the Native people for the destruction their churches had participated in. That council acknowledged how their churches had destroyed Native beliefs and how they really never did anything to help the Native people. They are a little bit late, but better late than never. Perhaps this is a dawning, a beginning of some positive way of reapproaching Native people. It might indicate that some people are willing to ask what they can do to help Native people rather than telling them what they should do to fit in with the technological society. It might be a step in the right direction.

In all the times that I've listened to the clergy, I've heard only a precious few express a willingness to help people go and find their own vision on the planet. I've seen only a few of them helping people to get their own power and become whole, balanced human beings. Such teaching is totally foreign to most advocates of technological religions.

We have to look very carefully at what is called the religion of submission. It seems to have always meant submission of the gentle to the aggressive, by the sword if necessary.

It's interesting that the societies that have been most destructive to the Earth Mother have also been the ones to keep women submissive. The Moslems don't do anything for the Earth; their philosophy doesn't contain anything that deals with the Earth. And it contains a lot about women being servants. The message of Islam is one of destruction of life. Judeo-Christian thought is similar in some ways, although these churches are trying a lot harder today. But most religions find it difficult to reach beyond the master/slave mentality.

Many Native people believe proponents of technological religions are destroying the planet because these religions have taken people away from their consciousness of the Earth. These religions have said that the Earth is "a veil of tears; a place of suffering." You hear people saying, "When I shed my mantle . . ." or "When I shed my envelope and go to heaven . . ."

This is the kind of conditioning that we must fight. This is the conditioning that is destroying the Earth. As an old Indian once said, "The white man always wants to go to heaven. I wish he'd go to heaven and leave the Earth for us Indians."

You need to look at this conditioning because of men like James Watt, who was Ronnie Reagan's right-hand man in the Department of Interior for a while. His idea was to use up everything on the Earth because, according to Watt, we don't have to worry about the Earth since it is going to be destroyed anyway, and all the good Christians will go to heaven.

Watt had no sense of respect for the Earth Mother or the creation. Many people do not have that respect. They have the idea that the Earth Mother is not our home, that it isn't a place where we belong. This mentality is causing the destruction of the planet. Understanding and breaking free from that mentality is an essential part of what we need to do.

We have to look at the governments of the world. We have to examine governmental policies for dealing with the Earth. We also have to look at how countries deal with other peoples in terms of their relationship to the Earth.

The whole perspective of the developed nations and big business toward the Earth has been one of total exploitation around the globe. Multinational corporations have no concept of the Earth as a living, intelligent being that is our mother. They have no respect for Earth's natural resources. They mine a natural resource to the last ounce and then leave great piles of mining tailings behind them. They aren't at all concerned with leaving these great scars upon the Earth. We really need to look at this approach.

In Africa, the multinationals have destroyed vast forests. We can see the results — the stumps, the sand and the desert — as millions of acres become part of the Sahara. When you look at a map of Africa now, only a very small portion of the land is capable of growing crops. The rest of it is turning into desert. The multinationals have kept cutting down the trees, with no regard for how this would affect the African people and their land.

At one time, all the African nations were the colonies of Christian nations — countries that went in there to steal everything they could. Portugal had its hands deep in Africa. Most other European countries also had their hands in there, for the sole purpose of exploitation. First they would take the minerals and natural resources out of the land, then they would abandon the land and the people without being concerned about what happened to either. If the people starved to death, that was tough. All that mattered to the exploiters was supply and demand. This exploitation has left entire countries in Africa without any source of income.

The attitude of the developed countries was that they always knew best; their activities were always for the Africans' own good. They also assumed they knew best how to solve the problems they created. For example, the technological nations went into Africa and said, "We will teach you the green revolution. We have these hybrids, these grains that are going to produce crops for you." They gave the Africans the hybrid seeds, which produced for maybe a couple of years. But in order to raise these crops, the developed nations went into Africa with bulldozers and tore up the thin, fragile layer of topsoil on which the Africans had raised their crops and animals for thousands of years. Now you see rust on the bulldozers over there, and starving people.

Those Africans with money to invest were lured by developers into drilling wells. This caused the water level to drop until there was no more water in some places. The corporations went into many areas, completely exploiting them in various ways, and then moved on.

Now they're doing the same thing in Brazil, Peru and other South American countries. Thousands and thousands of acres of rain forest are being stripped every year — all to make money. There isn't any kind of balance involved.

There was always a sadness in the Natives of North America and elsewhere because the "developed" people didn't listen to them. The Europeans who came to America had the opportunity to come into loving harmony and to gain the knowledge that would bring them into balance with creation, by sharing with the people who were already on the continent, blending their knowledge and their power. According to Native prophecies, if the Europeans didn't do this, the Indians would lie upon the face of the Earth as if dead in the dust for a hundred years or more. Then the power would come back to us.

This is what's happening now. People are coming by the thousands and studying the sacred ways. It is very powerful to see. People are listening now to Native people from many parts of the world because they look around and see the destruction that civilized humans have put upon the Earth. There are so many sad, glaring examples.

The coyote is very truly my brother. I say that because the Native people of the world have survived, not because of civilization but in spite of it, like the coyote. You need to learn from the coyote too. If you learn to hear and feel as a part of nature, you'll have a much better chance to make it through the changes into the Bright Day.

So many people today don't hear the Earth, yet she is talking to us all the time. The Earth is talking to us but most people have become deaf to her voice. When people see me call for the rains, they think it is *super*-natural, but in fact it is perfectly natural. I encourage people to begin their day by thanking Creator for the gift of life and the beauty all around. In this way they can begin to hear and feel the natural world once again.

Chapter Two

Prophetic Voices

Before any major change has ever occurred on this planet, there have been warnings. These warnings are what people call prophecies. There are many Native prophecies concerning events that are now happening upon the Earth. For example, there is the Iroquois prophecy spoken of by Mad Bear Anderson that tells about the wrestling of the serpents. Then there are the Hopi prophecies which tell about the four worlds, and the fifth one we may be preparing to enter. Among the Blackfoot Indians there is a prophecy staff that records prophecies similar to the one of the four worlds shared by the Hopi and other tribes.

Many tribes and peoples have prophecies that speak of Earth changes, and the things that are coming. Nostradamus wrote of such times and the powerful things which could happen. The Bible records events that came to pass as they were prophesied. In the Bible, as well as the historical records of other cultures, is the story of a great flood that came upon the Earth and caused the destruction of all of the people who were then living. It says some people were rescued, along with two each of all the animals. The warning about this flood was given by God to the people of that time through a teacher named Noah and his sons. According to the Biblical story, of all the tribal peoples of that time, only Noah and his family took the warning seriously. They were saved because they took the sacred path and listened to the warning of God, the Great Spirit.

Be aware. There is always a warning. The Bible also speaks in the Book of Revelation and the Book of Matthew about the ending of this current world. The Bible uses a Greek word which, according to what I have been able to understand, means the end of a system of things, not the end of the Earth. The Earth "abideth forever," according to the Bible. A similar statement shows up in Native prophecies. To me these statements mean there is nothing wrong with the Earth, but only with a certain number of humans who have gotten off the track and are destroying themselves, their fellow human beings, and life on Earth.

Native records written in stone are now known as petroglyphs or pictographs. There is a series of petroglyphs which I have seen that show major Earth changes happening in different places. After each sequence of events, there is a spiral that means "and life continues." This is what I feel also: Life will continue on this planet. There will be human survivors. These human survivors will be the ones who have reached a higher level of consciousness and are willing to move on and take responsibility for themselves and for the planet in a sacred manner.

Remember well that before any major change happens on this planet, there are warnings. A story I've heard says that back in the 1930's there was a small band of Indians living in a valley in California. One day, they packed up and left the area. Their neighbors around them asked, "What's happening? Why are you leaving?" The Indians said, "Big water coming soon." This was during a dry spell and the neighbors said, "Oh, you funny Indians! What do you mean, big water coming soon?"

Two weeks later a dam burst and flooded the valley. The Indian people left the valley because they had had a warning, and they heeded it. They saw their relatives — their little animal brothers and sisters — all going to higher ground. They knew something was going to happen. So when the dam burst, they weren't caught in the flood.

In 1973 in Bangladesh there were spiritual leaders, medicine people, who tried to warn their people that a catastrophe was coming. These leaders told the people to evacuate a certain area because there was a great tidal wave coming. Many people didn't listen to them. Two weeks later a tidal wave came and flooded the whole area, drowning some 500,000 people. These people died because they weren't willing to listen. A warning had been given to them.

We have to be willing to listen. Many things make sense if you listen to the Earth, or to the prophets of the Earth. Native people have always advocated listening to the Earth. This is something we feel very strongly about. Before any catastrophe happens, we sense it.

Back in 1976, I was on the Bear Tribe land in Washington State. I started seeing all the animals going to higher country. I told my people that something powerful was going to happen, some powerful destructive force was going to let loose. A couple of weeks later, a dam burst in Idaho and caused flooding for 150 miles. Luckily, we weren't affected, but the behavior of the animals had warned me that something major was going to happen.

Native prophecies from all the lands, and the spiritual teachers of many different peoples, speak of things that will happen at this time. They speak of major changes. They speak of people who will survive, human beings who will want to take a sacred path in harmony with the Earth. They say that those who do so will stay alive even though there will come a time of great destruction to the Earth. The wise people will know what to do and will move in a sacred manner to make the changes necessary for their own survival and for the survival of others. Those who do survive will be the people who have studied the prophecies and have learned how to hear the Earth.

Earth Spirits Reborn

I'm going to share with you a prophecy of my own people, the Ojibwa. This is a prophecy told to us by our great ancestors through our pictographs. They saw the coming of the Europeans to this continent. They saw the kind of hats they would be wearing. They saw how they would look and the kind of canoes they would have. They were told that if these people came in a sacred manner and accepted the knowledge that was given to them by the people of this continent, then it would be a beautiful thing. We would walk as brothers and sisters on the land.

It soon became obvious that the Europeans didn't respect the sacred teachings of the land. Our prophecies said that if this happened, there would come a time when we would lie in the dust for 100 years or more as if we were

29

dead. Even our own people wouldn't respect our teachings, and both Native and non-Native people would fail to understand them. Some Natives would turn from the teachings and be lured away saying, "This is a better teaching."

Our prophecies also said that at the end of that 100 years, we would be walking on our hind legs again. We would be alive as if we were Earth spirits just reborn. We'd stand up and have our power again. We would be able to call in the forces — the thunder and the lightning and the storms — and communicate with these powers all the time because this is part of our ancient knowledge. We would have these abilities again, and we would return to the sacred path.

At that time, our sons and daughters would again come to us and ask to be taught the sacred ways. And the sons and daughters of the people who had come across the Great Water would come to us, too. They would say, "Teach us, for we are about to destroy the Earth." This is the stage we are at right now.

When this prophecy was first shared with us by our people, we wondered how anyone could destroy the Earth. Now we know. We see how the planet-hating ones are ruining the Earth.

Dreams Of Destruction

Over a period of time I have had many, many dreams that showed the coming of the Earth changes. I've dreamed of things that would happen before they happened. I've had these dreams and so have other people. One reason that I organized the Bear Tribe as a rural-based community was because I saw in my dreams major destruction coming to the cities.

I saw a time when the cities wouldn't exist in their present state. During the changes the most dangerous places will be near cities with nuclear and chemical plants. But all major cities will experience a breakdown in services. In my dreams, I've seen great garbage piles on the streets, the

30

electric service out of order because of storms and earthquakes, broken water mains, and no more gasoline because of a major breakdown of the system.

I also foresee race riots in the big cities, with street gangs engaged in uncontrolled fighting against each other, using guns to get what they want. When there is no money to pay their salaries, the police will not be there to protect the people in the city. Instead, in one of my dreams, I saw the police banded together in groups calling themselves "Brothers of the Gun." They were using their guns to take whatever they wanted. This is already happening in other parts of the world. In Peru, for instance, I know one American man who was handcuffed and robbed by men dressed like police in the men's room of the Lima airport. These men — whether police or not — took his money, watch, and camera and left him with $20 to get home.

I see the cities being hit by major epidemics caused by bad water, toxic chemicals, or other things. Currently, in the southwestern United States, the bubonic plague is being spread by the fleas on ground squirrels. If these fleas spread to the rat population of the major cities, then we will have big problems. Bubonic plague was called the "Black Death" of the Middle Ages in Europe. Fifty million people died from this disease. The call of the people in the villages then was, "Bring out your dead." The people would haul the corpses away and burn them, hoping to stop the spread of the death. Today we also have the pneumonic plague, which is even worse than the bubonic. Pneumonic plague is spread by the germ-carrying mucous of infected people as they cough and sneeze on others.

In my dreams, I've also seen wheat crops that had rusted. They had candy-like clumps of rust, a serious disease that was destroying the crops. There were great black birds like crows or vultures, just waiting. With nothing left to eat, these birds were scavenging bodies as humans died.

I once shared this dream with a man who is a research agriculturalist. He said, "You are seeing the truth, Sun Bear.

We have diseases among crops now that we can't control. They run wild and we can't control them. They go from field to field across the country in some places. Up in Idaho, there are places where they can't raise their great potato and onion crops because there's a particular disease that causes each new crop to rot."

Back in 1973, throughout the southern United States, there was a major corn smut that caused the farmers to lose three fourths of their crops. The smut went from one field to another, destroying thousands and thousands of acres. This is something that happens, particularly with hybrids because they have so little immunity. In my dreams I see diseases like this continuing to cause great destruction.

In the early 1980's in my workshops and writings, I spoke of major earthquakes striking Russia prior to the year 2000. In the late 1980's, these earthquakes began happening. I've also spoken often of a dream I had in 1978, in which I saw a map of Iran. In the dream, the word "Iran" vanished off the map. Spirit told me the dream meant that Iran would eventually be destroyed by its neighbors and by earthquakes. This destruction has begun. Throughout most of the 1980's, Iran was involved in a devastating war with Iraq. Now major earthquakes have hit Iran; as recently as June 1990 a large earthquake killed more than 50,000 people and left many times that number homeless. As of late 1990, tensions continued between Iran and its neighbors, and scientists were predicting that more and larger earthquakes may strike the area. So this is the way that dreams can show us what will happen.

In my dreams I've also seen small bands of people living very close to the Earth. I saw that other people would come to join them, and they would embrace these newcomers. All they said to them was, "You have survived." There were no "isms" left in the world — not Catholicism, not Communism, nothing. We were all just human beings living on the Earth in a sacred manner.

Once when I was in Germany I had a dream where I

was in a forest. I found a wolf skull with rotting flesh and hair. I cleaned off the flesh and hair with my fingers. I asked Spirit what this meant. Spirit told me that the skull represented the ancient spirits of Germany. Then Spirit said that there were still political people among the Germans who would try to cause destruction. But after these people were cleaned out, the rest of the German people would come back to their true spiritual path and walk in a sacred manner.

A year later, I was in Germany again to do a workshop. A woman came up to me before the workshop began. She said that she had had a powerful dream. In it, she saw a wolf skull and was told it symbolized the ancient spirits of Germany. Spirit often speaks the same words to different people.

Many of the things that give me direction come through Spirit in dreams. I know the dream time is very important. It's the time when you shut off your everyday mind. As a result, you're able to open up to Spirit. It's the time when Spirit can communicate messages and knowledge.

In Australia, the Aboriginal people are famous for their dreaming. They say they have 40,000 years of dreamtime as part of their sacred teachings. They dream of their children before they're born; they dream which sex they'll be and what their personalities will be like. They have special places where they go to pray for their dreaming.

When I visited there, the Aborigines asked me to dream for them. So I prayed for a dream, and in it, I saw a place near the ocean where there was a great sand dune. Behind that, I saw a place where there was lower land. I told them I saw a rising and a sinking and that a part of their land would be flooded. They agreed, saying they already knew about that from their own dreams.

Many times people will tell me about dreams similar to my own, or I'll dream about a major disaster, and then it happens. For example, I had a dream in December of 1988 in which I saw two airplanes catch on fire in midair.

Within three weeks, a TWA airplane exploded over Scotland because of a bomb; shortly thereafter, a British Airways airplane caught fire and crashed. This is why I believe very strongly in the power of seeing things with dreams. I encourage people to pray for dreams and allow Spirit to tell them things before they happen.

Piercing The Veil

There is another prophecy which is spoken of on our migration scrolls. This one tells about the four worlds, which are represented by four circles drawn on birch bark. Inside each circle are shown all the things that would happen to humankind, all the changes and the powerful ideas that would come during each particular world.

There is a bear in each circle with his tongue sticking out. The interpretation of this is that the bear pierces the veil of the next world with his tongue in order to bring the people the knowledge they need to move into the next world. I had been teaching for well over five years before I really understood that prophecy. I believe that what I have been doing with my teaching is piercing the veil of the fifth world, helping to take us into that world by sharing knowledge with people to help them come free from this fourth world we are living in now. By sharing knowledge of the prophecies and Earth changes, I show people glimpses of the next world.

I have had visions of these times of Earth changes and of what is necessary to survive them. I feel a responsibility to share knowledge with the people who are ready for it, who open themselves up to it. If they are not ready to hear, then there is nothing I can do.

Until 1970 I worked only with Native people. Then the Great Spirit told me the time of the changes was near, and I had to go out and speak to all people, Native and non-Native alike. I followed Spirit's direction and, indeed, since the early 1970's, the changes have been building momentum.

Another prophecy of my Native people speaks of a time when the Earth would hold back her increase: one area would be too wet; another, too dry. One place would be too hot; another, too cold. This is what we are experiencing now. Over the past few years, much of the news is about a drought here, a record cold somewhere else, and heat waves in another location. A few years back, crops valued at over four billion dollars were lost to drought in the Southeast. At the same time in the Midwest, rivers flooded, causing tremendous crop damage of a different kind.

Another part of the prophecy states that the rivers will change their courses. When the Missouri River flooded over in the late 1980's, it did in fact start a new channel. These events are just a small part of the prophecies that are becoming a reality today.

At one time there was a great prophet in Ohio named Tenskwatawa. He was the twin brother of Techumseh, the famous Shawnee chief, and was called The Prophet. Prophetstown, Ohio, is named after him. Back in the early 1800's, Tenskwatawa had warned the people that if they didn't respond to Tecumseh's message and support him in what he was doing, he would stomp his foot and the ground would shake as far south as Florida! And this is what happened. At the time The Prophet predicted it, there was a major earthquake in Missouri, the biggest one in American history. Once, in a dream, The Prophet's daughter visited me. It was a very powerful experience. She told me the time would come when major earthquakes would again affect areas in the midwestern United States.

In A Sacred Manner

Many years ago, around 1953, Daddy Brae, a Kahuna medicine man from Hawaii, said that when the Earth changes were in process, two volcanoes would erupt at the same time. This happened in 1984 when both Mauna Kea and Kilauea erupted simultaneously.

Then there is an old monk of the Hindu faith who told me his people have a prophecy that says the Earth changes would begin when the trees started to die. This is happening now all throughout Europe. In areas of Germany, more than half of the trees are dead or dying. Trees are also dying in increasingly large parts of the United States and Canada. They are dying from the tops down from acid rain and other pollutants.

Another of the prophecies says that there will come a time when people will not be able to go out of their houses because of the poisons in the air. I was in Germany when the Chernobyl nuclear disaster occurred in Russia. Just as the prophecy said, people were warned not to go outside of their houses because of the radioactive fallout.

The winter of 1988, two years after the Chernobyl disaster, saw the worst cold on record in Russia and Europe. The two events are connected. We humans are creating the Earth changes along with nature. Humankind is a part of all of this.

The sacred teachings all show that we are definitely moving into major Earth changes now. The prophecies are being fulfilled. We are at the end of one era and the beginning of a new one. Although the Earth changes are part of a foretold sequence, they are coming more quickly because of the human role in them. During these times, it will be difficult for our Earth Mother to preserve herself from destruction at the hand of humankind. The Earth has gone through major changes throughout her history. The difference now is the influence of humans, escalating the speed and severity of what is happening.

My people see this time of great change as a period of cleansing and moving forward. Humankind is being given a great opportunity to make a major breakthrough in consciousness and awareness. The people who are going to survive the changes, according to what I've understood, are those who are reaching out to a higher level of awareness, an awareness that lets them walk in a more sacred manner. When we go into the next level of the change, what we call the fifth level — the present being the fourth one — only those people who walk sacredly will be part of the Bright Day.

In the fifth world we will be able to live more in harmony with the Earth and each other. This is what we are being prepared for by the changes, and by the many teachers who are among us even now. In the fifth world, those people who spend their time trying to destroy the Earth and each other will no longer be around.

I see about one fourth of the world's population surviving. All those who do survive will come through with a higher level of consciousness. I believe, and so do other Native people, that there will be great spiritual teachers coming to us. Some of them are here already. These teachers will be helping to guide humanity through the time of the changes. After that, we will have a totally different sense of what it's all about. So this is a time of cleansing, on many levels, and there are going to be many things that are here now that will no longer be around when the cleansing is completed.

Little Sister Speaks

I live in the state of Washington. The Native people there have a prophecy that came to them a long time back. This prophecy said a time would come when the Little Sister would speak and the Grandfather would answer, and the land would be swept clean to the ocean. In December of 1979 a medicine brother of mine packed up and moved his people inland from the west coast of Washington, near a place called Spirit Lake, to Idaho, some 70 miles from where I live. He told me that the time had come for the prophecy to be fulfilled. The mountain that we call the Little Sister is called Mt. St. Helens in geography books.

In December, 1979, Mt. St. Helens was still considered a dormant volcano by geologists. In March of 1980, the Little Sister began to whisper. On May 18th of 1980, the

Little Sister spoke and threw a cubic mile of mountain into the air, covering the whole Northwest, and eventually the globe, with volcanic ash. Sixty-seven people who didn't believe in the Indian prophecy are buried beneath the mountain near a place that was called Spirit Lake.

Some of us recognized the eruption for what it was — part of the cleansing, the Earth renewal. When the Little Sister spoke, we acknowledged it as the power of the Creator coming through.

That year the Bear Tribe had planted its gardens the same as always. We also planted a pasture for our livestock. We walked over the land throwing grass seed by hand because we didn't have any high-priced equipment. It's called "broadcasting the seed." We were praying for rain to help the seed take root. The Creator did us one better — one inch of topsoil fell from the heavens, and then it rained. We had the best pasture we've ever had and gardens that produced 45 percent more than they ever had before. We had to build another root cellar that year because we had so much more food to store. The ash regenerated the land in eastern Washington that had become dead from years of misuse. It was truly a re-creation of the Earth.

The other part of this Northwest prophecy — the Grandfather will answer, and the land will be swept clean to the ocean — is also very powerful.

In 1986 I did a workshop in Seattle with Sondra Ray, creator of the Loving Relationships workshop and author of several books. She invited me to do a ceremony on Mt. Rainier. A forest ranger was there, telling a group of tourists about Mt. Rainier and all the different ice caves within it. Then he said, "There's an Indian prophecy about this mountain and about Mt. St. Helens. The Indians said that Little Sister (Mt. St. Helens) would speak and Grandfather (Mt. Rainier) would answer, and the land would be swept clean to the ocean."

About three months earlier, according to the ranger,

two steam vents appeared on Mt. Rainier, so he knew it was alive. I feel that it's going to blow before the year 2000, and, when it does, it will go toward the ocean. According to the prophecy, it will sweep the land clean to the ocean. A funny thing about volcanoes is that they don't care who claims the land; they can repossess it. They just move in and take it.

The Northwest Indians who predicted the eruption of Mt. St. Helens had some other very powerful prophets. One was Chief Sealth — popularly known as Chief Seattle — of the Suquamish tribe. His prophecies are contained in one of his speeches, made around 1853, that is among the most well-known Indian talks ever given. In it he speaks of a time when the white man would come to the Northwest and diminish the Native people. He says:

We know that the white man does not understand our ways. One portion of the land is the same to him as the next, for he is a stranger who comes in the night and takes from the land whatever he needs. The Earth is not his brother, but his enemy, and when he has conquered it, he moves on. . . . His appetite will devour the Earth and leave behind only a desert.

The air is precious to the red man, for all things share the same breath — the beast, the tree, the man — they all share the same breath. The white man does not seem to notice the air he breathes. Like a man dying for many days, he is numb to the stench . . .

. . . I have seen a thousand rotting buffaloes on the prairie, left by the white man who shot them from a passing train. I am a savage and I do not understand how the smoking iron horse can be more important than the buffalo we kill only to stay alive.

What is man without beasts? If all the beasts were gone, man would die from a great loneliness of spirit. For whatever happens to the beasts, soon happens to man. All things are connected.

. . . Teach your children what we have taught our

children, that the Earth is our mother. Whatever befalls the Earth befalls the sons of the Earth. If men spit upon the ground, they spit upon themselves.

This we know: The Earth does not belong to man; man belongs to the Earth. This we know. All things are connected like the blood which unites one family. All things are connected.

Whatever befalls the Earth befalls the sons of the Earth. Man did not weave the thread of life; he is merely a strand in it. Whatever he does to the web, he does to himself.

Even the white man, whose God walks and talks with him as friend to friend, cannot be exempt from the common destiny. We may be brothers after all. We shall see. One thing we know, which the white man may one day discover — Our God is the same God. You may think now that you own Him as you wish to own our land; but you cannot. He is the God of man, and His compassion is equal for the red man and the white. This Earth is precious to Him, and to harm the Earth is to heap contempt on its Creator. The whites too shall pass; perhaps sooner than all other tribes. Contaminate your bed, and you will one night suffocate in your own waste.

But in your perishing you will shine brightly, fired by the strength of the God who brought you to this land and for some special purpose gave you dominion over this land and over the red man. That destiny is a mystery to us, for we do not understand when the buffalo are all slaughtered, the wild horses are tamed, the secret corners of the forest heavy with the scent of many men, and the view of the ripe hills blotted by talking wires. Where is the thicket? Gone. Where is the eagle? Gone. The end of living and the beginning of survival.

Another great visionary was named Smohalla. He founded the "Washani," or seven-drum religion, and warned his people of the coming of the "Upsuch," the greedy ones. He told his people to keep the old ways if they wanted to survive. They listened too late. But some of Smohalla's dreams were kept alive by one of his students — Wovoka, the ghost dance messiah. Wovoka taught many Indian people that if they kept dancing and dreaming spring would come and the Earth would be reborn.

Wrestling Serpents

Another prophecy that has come to fulfillment is from the Iroquois people. This prophecy was given to me by a spiritual man of the Iroquois named Mad Bear Anderson, who told me to share it with people. I've been telling about this prophecy of the wrestling serpents since 1973.

Among the Iroquois, the spiritual people and their medicine societies have staffs. On some of these staffs, there are three serpents. There's a white and a red serpent with the same tail. This indicates they have the same purpose toward humanity: domination, conquest, and control. The prophecy given me by Mad Bear Anderson says that the white and red serpents would wrestle until the rivers boiled and the fish turned up dead. Then a black serpent would come and wrestle with and defeat both the white and the red serpent. Then he would look around to see if there were other people to fight with. He would see the Native people gathered in the hilly country, along with all the other people who gathered with them wanting to understand the spiritual way of the Earth. He would turn as if to fight with them, but then he would see coming the great light of Deganawida, the great teacher of the Northeast Indian people. He would become frightened, flee and never bother the people again.

The interpretation of this prophecy, given to me by Spirit, is that the white and red serpents represent the United States and the Soviet Union. They wrestled for a long time, until the rivers boiled and the fish turned up dead from their atomic weapons testing. They wrestled in the Cold War, supplying armaments to get other people to fight against each other. They wrestled until they exhausted almost all their resources, until they were in so much debt from their wrestling they couldn't afford to continue anymore. This is the stage we're at right now.

Then the black serpent comes into the battle. The black serpent is the Moslem nations. The Moslem nations have gotten both the United States and the Soviet Union into wars they didn't know how to fight. They defeated the United States in Lebanon and the Soviets in Afghanistan. Neither country knows how to battle this black serpent.

Now we're coming into the second stage of the wrestling of serpents: the war of the Moslem nations. This war can affect all the nations of the world. In it, the battlefield will be the gas pumps. It will drain the last dollar from those countries that have become overly dependent on oil for the life blood of their economies. The Moslem nations control most of the world's petroleum; they can make quite a noose for Western Civilization from their fuel lines.

In late 1990 Iraq continued its occupation of Kuwait, and remained a major power in the Arab/oil world. This clearly begins the fulfillment of this stage of the prophecy.

The Four Worlds

Powerful prophecies have been brought to me by other people, including an old man of the Hopi people named Soloho. Soloho was a powerful healer who did things similar to what the Filipino psychic surgeons do. He had that kind of power. He also had the knowledge of the Hopi prophecies. Only two clans of the Hopi have knowledge of all the prophecies, while different villages have parts of them. Before he passed on, Soloho said to me, "Now you can share these with other people." I tell these prophecies the way he told me to tell them. Some Hopi or other teachers may tell them differently, but this is what he told me.

He gave me an eagle feather and said, "This is my gift to you. Because this feather comes from the breast of the eagle, it represents the life force of the eagle, and the breast represents the ability to transmit the knowledge. This is what you must take out to the people."

The Hopi speak of four worlds. The first was a world in which the Creator placed human beings. As long as they kept in balance and in harmony, they were permitted to continue living there. When they got out of harmony with the Spirit, Spirit called for a cleansing. Those people who were willing to keep the sacred path were told to go into the Earth, that they would be protected there. The place where they went down into the Earth was at the Grand Canyon, the place of emergence. It's a hole that goes right down into the ground. Nobody knows how deep it goes. (Another one like it was discovered in Arizona. This one is called a "breather hole" for the planet and there's a wind coming up from it all the time.) The people of the first world were told to go down in the hole and to take food with them, so that they would be safe there during the time of the cleansing. Then the Creator called for the volcanoes to erupt. Volcanoes erupted, throwing volcanic rock all over the area. The eruptions also caused gasses to spread over the land. These killed everybody who wasn't down in the hole. The people stayed in the hole for as long as the Creator told them to.

When it was over, they came out again and repopulated Earth. This was the second world. People lived in it longer than they had before. Then they lost their balance again. They thought they had all the answers, and they stopped listening to Spirit. The Creator again called for a cleansing. This time the spirit-keepers who protect the North and South Poles were asked to leave their places and let Earth spin free. And Earth spun free. This was a pole shift. Great winds tore at the planet and great icefields came over it. It was a very powerful cleansing.

Up until that time, the soft spot we have on top of our

heads when we're babies stayed open all during our lifetime. But after this cleansing, Creator sealed it over because the human race was not ready to seek the sacred path. From then on, knowledge would come a little harder.

In the third world people populated Earth even more widely than they had before. They had gained much more knowledge and many more skills by this time. They built great cities and machines capable of doing many things, including machines that could fly. They waged war between the cities, and they set up boundaries over the land and proclaimed pieces of it as belonging to one person or tribe. They developed crystals and used them for destructive purposes. They invented forms of lasers that were also capable of destruction. The Spirit saw all this sickness.

Again, the Creator called for a cleansing. This time the call was for the waters of the oceans to rise and waters to come down from the heavens. This cleansing was a great flood. Then the people who were going to survive on this continent — a man and his two sons and their families — were put into a state of suspended animation and sealed up in hollow tubes. They floated upon the water until the waters receded. Then they came out onto the land. The father wanted to start some of the old practices again. The Creator just took him out of action right there; that was the end of it. The two brothers and their families wanted to follow the Creator's way. One was told to travel to the east and populate the lands, while the other one went to the west. The one who went west was the Hopi. The one who went east was called the True White Brother.

The Hopi were told that they would find the land where they should be. The Blue Star Kachina went before them. It danced in the sky, guiding them. When they came to the land where they live now, the Blue Star Kachina stopped. They knew this was their land. Then the Hopi were told they should journey, some to the west, some to the north, some to the south, and some to the east, and that what they brought back from those areas would become part of their path and their teachings. Among the Hopi in Arizona today, there are ceremonies related to parrots that they got in South America. And they have other strange ceremonial animals that came from other areas to which they journeyed.

They were told their land would be very harsh but that if they did the ceremonies they were supposed to do, the land would provide for them. They had to say the prayers and perform the ceremonies every year. They stayed on the land they had been given and planted their corn and prayed over it. They kept tilling the land, carrying a little water to it and producing a crop of the sacred corn every year. They were told to watch for the True White Brother. First the Spaniards came and the Hopi asked, "Are you the True White Brother?" The Spaniards said, "Where is the gold, where is the yellow iron?" And the Hopi knew they were not the one. When the other Europeans came, the Hopi asked, "Are you the True White Brother?" But these people only wanted to go to California, saying, "That's where the gold is. We're going there."

The Hopi have tablets of stone. On them are highlights of everything that is going to happen before the next cleansing. These tablets told the Hopi that people would come first with strange animals pulling boxes — wagon trains — and then the boxes would move by themselves — the trains and automobiles. They were told that a silver thread would be put across the land; this was Highway 66.

They were also told that they would see spider webs in the sky that people would talk through — the telephone and telegraph — and that the time would come when the eagle would walk on the moon. When the American astronaut, Neil Armstrong, stepped onto the moon from his spaceship and said, "Eagle has landed," it was the fulfillment of the Hopi prophecy.

The Hopi were told the time would come when two powers would shake the Earth twice. The symbol of one of them would be the rising sun — Japan — and the symbol of the other would be a sign of the four directions —

Germany. During World War I, the Germans used the Maltese Cross as their insignia; in World War II, they had the swastika, both symbols of the four directions. The Hopi were told that at the time of this great conflict, some power would pour a gourd of ashes from the heavens making the rivers boil and the fish turn up on their bellies. This was the atomic bomb.

The Hopi were told to journey to a place where all the nations of the world would be gathered and try to speak to them, warn them to return to sacred ways. They went four times to the United Nations building. Three times when they asked to go in, they weren't allowed. The fourth time my spiritual grandfather, Wallace Black Elk, went before them carrying a pipe. They were allowed through the door, but still they were able to talk to only a few of the delegates. They wouldn't let Black Elk or the Hopi address the entire General Assembly. The Hopi prophecies had told them that if this happened, the time of the cleansing was very near. So the Hopi returned to their land.

The Hopi were told the fourth cleansing could come about in two ways. One way would see all four elements called into action. This means that we would see great floods in many places, more powerful winds than we have seen before, the Earth shaking, and the great volcanoes erupting. We would be seeing earth, water, fire and air all being part of the cleansing. This is happening right now.

The other way the cleansing could come about would be by a people whose color was red. They would come over this land in one day and conquer it. If that happened, the Hopi were warned that nobody should go outside of their houses because there would be something in the air that would kill them.

I told this prophecy in late April of 1986 in Germany, and the next day there were some Germans who knew what the prophecy was about, because the nuclear disaster at Chernobyl happened. The Germans were told, for the next four days, not to go outside of their houses. I felt an

46

aching in my bones from Chernobyl. It's very powerful to be so close to that kind of destruction.

The Hopi were told that if there were people who would turn to the sacred ways, to the sacred teachings, these people would pass through and survive the cleansing. But if the people didn't come back into balance and harmony, then the insects would inherit the Earth. It's very interesting that insects have armor against atomic radiation. It's something in their shells called chitin that protects them.

The Hopi were also told that the Blue Star Kachina would return and dance in the village. Several years ago this happened. And the Hopi were told that their True White Brother would come to their land. In about 1984, the True White Brother came in the form of a people from a distant land where they also had prophecies.

The True White Brother had been told that the time would come when their land would be invaded and they would no longer be able to practice their teachings in a sacred manner. At that time, their prophecies told them to go to the land of the red man. These were the Tibetan people. I've sat with them, and we've shared knowledge. The Dalai Lama has visited with the Hopi. Our hearts are one in harmony. There are several places in the world where I use Tibetan centers for my lectures and workshops. There's a feeling between us; we feel the same sacred path. It is strong medicine.

The Hopi were told that after the cleansing the people who survived would perhaps keep the religion that they had; or perhaps seek another one; or, they might even have evolved to where they didn't need religion any more. One of the things I try to teach my apprentices in the Bear Tribe is to grow to that level of consciousness and power where they carry the law in their own hearts. To me, that's the ultimate goal: live so you don't need a policeman on every corner. Live in a way that you are centered and carry the law within your heart. That's strong medicine. As Bob Dylan sings, "To live outside of the law, one must be honest."

The Four Horsemen

The Biblical Book of Matthew says Jesus was asked what the signs would be that would show the time of his coming, and the end of the world. (Again, the Greek word used is the one for the end of a system, not the end of life). According to the Bible, Jesus answered that there would be wars and rumors of wars; that nation would rise against nation; kingdom against kingdom; and there would be famine, pestilence and earthquakes in many places.

In the sixth chapter of the Book of Revelation is the prophecy of the four horsemen of the apocalypse. This prophecy tells of the major events that would happen upon the Earth at the time of its cleansing. The four horsemen represent great powers that will come over the Earth. The first horseman sat upon a white horse and had the power to conquer. He was used for the destruction of people. The second horseman sat upon a red horse. The power given him was to take peace from the Earth, so that people would kill one another. This horseman was given a great sword. The third horseman sat upon a black horse, holding a pair of balances in his hand. A voice in the midst of the horsemen was heard to say, "A measure of wheat for a penny, and three measures of barley for a penny. And see that they spare not the oil and the wine." Biblical scholars translate this to mean that there will be very high prices for everything, likely as the result of drought and famine. When the fourth horseman appeared, he rode a pale horse. The name of this horseman was Death, and Hell was said to follow him. This horseman was given powers to kill with a sword, with hunger, with illness and with the beasts of the Earth.

Throughout the Book of Revelation are mentioned great earthquakes that would strike the Earth and cause massive destruction. "Greater earthquakes than have ever been known before would strike." These things show up in ancient Biblical prophecies as events that will be happening when the Earth needs cleansing.

The Forward Leap

The Earth cleansing that we're experiencing now is necessary for the protection of the planet. It is also necessary because the purpose of humanity here on Earth is for each of us to go to our highest level of consciousness and power, and then learn how to apply the knowledge we gain in the process.

This is a time when humankind has to make the leap forward. The change we need to make is not something that is "kind of nice to do." We have to consciously make a leap forward if we're going to survive.

As this knowledge begins to come to you, it's your responsibility to dig deeper. Once you can touch a different level of consciousness, you begin to feel its reality and to know it's your obligation to start uncovering more. That's what it's about at this time: discovering more knowledge to help people survive during the time of changes.

We need to recover what we can of the knowledge that was stolen from us or kept from us. Gathering that knowledge together now is necessary for the people's survival. All of the prophecies of the Native people are being fulfilled at this time.

For me, the Earth changes are happening at a very comfortable pace; I have no problem with them. I'm not where the volcano goes off. When the river overflows its banks, I'm up there waving at the ice floes as they go by. Spirit has told me where to be and where not to be.

Knowing where to be is part of the process. That's why I publish the magazine *Wildfire*, and that's why I'm doing all the other things I do. I'm trying to reach out and help create a larger group of people who are in harmony with the Earth. These people won't get wiped out in the process of the Earth changes. If you know where to be and how to prepare, this can be a very comfortable, interesting, and exciting time.

Chapter Three

The Earth Changes Are Here

The Earth changes are here. I am glad they are. They're necessary for the survival of the planet. This is what we Indians were told long ago and what Spirit tells us today. These changes are a time of cleansing. Right now, the Earth is like a great big shaggy dog and humans are like fleas in its hair. When the dog starts shaking we get very worried, as well we should. We've been living in this changing time since 1973. According to all my beliefs, the changes will go on past the year 2000 with ever increasing intensity.

The reason that the Earth changes are happening, and will continue to happen, is because many humans are not yet willing to make the necessary changes in themselves and their actions which could prevent them. They are not willing to stop polluting and to start moving in a sacred manner. They will not stop throwing their garbage all over the planet.

A while back, I went out to a park where there used to be a sanctuary for animals. I heard this "clang, clang" noise. I looked for the source and saw a skunk with her head caught in a tin can. I knew she'd die if I didn't help her. I also knew of her potential to make me smell pretty bad. But I risked it. I grabbed her tail by one hand and braced the can between two bushes, pulled her out of it and turned her loose. That saved her life. She could have died due to the stupidity of someone who didn't pick up their garbage.

I'm told that the Japanese use 40-mile "drift nets" out in the ocean to catch squid. But the nets also catch other kinds of creatures. They're nylon nets so they last forever; they don't rot like the old cotton type. Sometimes, the Japanese lose a drift net and it goes on catching and killing creatures in the ocean. The people who lost it don't bother to look for it, even though it's wiping out the creatures they're depending on for food, and for life. These people don't take any responsibility for tomorrow.

To Native people, the Earth is a living, intelligent being. It is capable of making the necessary changes for its own survival. These changes might not be convenient for humans, but the Earth will make them anyway. There will be drastic climatic changes, earthquakes, volcanic eruptions, economic and political problems, and other problems humankind has caused for itself. The planet will survive, even though perhaps millions of people will perish. The predictions of different people vary regarding how many people will survive the cleansing. Some people say that up to 75 percent of the present population will perish; others say 90 percent. Whatever the number will be, we're looking at a vast change in worldwide population, and a lot of death.

I repeat, so you will remember: Humans are just another species on the planet. We are the same as deer and other creatures that begin to die off when they get too far out of balance, or out of harmony with the path they're supposed to be on.

When things become too disharmonious, the Creator and the spirit powers that work with the planet start things in motion to regain a planetary balance. Using the Earth-web, they create a chain of events that bring about major changes, making things uncomfortable for humans trying to survive in certain areas, forcing them to leave those areas.

If you go to the Southwest, you will find places like Lost City, Nevada, or Chaco Canyon, Arizona. In previous times, there used to be thousands of people in these areas. They had to move on because they lost their respect for the Earth and fell out of balance. They started fighting among themselves.

Creator said, "Well, they're so busy killing each other off that we'll give them something else to think about." So a natural disaster would occur and make them remove themselves from the area. Those who survived were a little more humble afterwards. They had been forced to put aside some of their arrogance. So it's something that is necessary, these Earth changes, because we're not doing enough to make the necessary changes by ourselves.

Back in the 1970's, there was a study published called "The Year 2000 Report." It was prepared during the Carter administration and it reported on what the world would be like in the year 2000. It showed that by then there would be major water shortages, most of the forests would be gone, and there would be many areas suffering from severe famine. This report was a frightening but accurate portrayal of what humans were doing to the Earth. It should have sparked immediate changes in policy by all governments on the planet. Instead, they ignored or denied it.

The year 2000 is still a few years off, but already many of these things are close on the horizon. An area the size of Massachusetts is becoming desert every year. An area two thirds that size is denuded of forests each year. The rain forests of the Amazon are being cut at the rate of 51 acres each minute. The Amazon region produces 40 percent of the oxygen in the world. So, we're getting worse air every day because of what is happening there.

In the United States the water table is dropping at a rate of one and a half feet per year. In some areas, it's dropping at a rate of nine feet per year. And there are three million acres of land being put under freeways, subdivisions and shopping centers each year. We're losing a lot of our good agricultural and forest land to this "development."

We have used pesticides to such an extent that some 400 species of insects are now totally immune to all the current pesticides. However, the pesticides have worked very well in the destruction of other wildlife. Grasshopper poison in ten Western states has killed off many of the natural grasshopper predators like sparrow hawks and meadowlarks. They die from eating the poisoned insects. Meanwhile, the grasshoppers are doing fine. And when I drive across the western United States, I see ponds that used to have ducks, frogs, and other wildlife. I look now and they're not there anymore; all the wildlife is dead. Instead, I see great chemical tanks containing herbicides, pesticides and fertilizers sitting on top of the hills, waiting to dump their poisons upon the land and into the water. This is what is happening.

What Is

We are also told that at the time of the cleansing, the spirit beings will materialize, take form again, and that they will be here to help humans, to teach and guide us directly. We are told we will have constant instruction to help us grow to our fullest level of consciousness and power. We humans need this so we won't be going off in wrong directions. ˑ''Touched by an Angel''

Individually, we are of different ages. But people who are responding to the knowledge that I'm sharing are all the same age. I say this because many Native people feel that those people living now who are looking at life in a real way will survive after the year 2000. We've come into the same level of consciousness, and we are very much aware of *what is happening* and what is going to happen. So we are Bright Day people, those who may live to have very different lives.

Recently I was thinking about the changes. I said, "Creator Spirit, what am I doing here? What am I really doing here? I represent a totally different philosophy than what this society espouses. I'm looking at a whole society that believes technology and progress is the answer. That sure isn't my opinion."

The dominant society worldwide has this one little direction that they're looking in for salvation. Spirit is telling me, a Native person, to stand in front of that society and say, "Hey, this isn't working, kids." I'm here to get people's attention and tell them that maybe they are going to have to look at life a different way. All those computers and all the armaments that governments have can't turn a killer snowstorm around; they can't stop an earthquake anywhere.

This is a time of very, very powerful changes on the Earth. It's a time that the Native people have been looking forward to because we know it is necessary for the survival of the planet. We know that humankind is still not willing to make the changes necessary for the survival of the planet, nor for the survival of the rest of the wild creatures who live on it. To give you an example, several states in the Southeast recently banned the catching of redfish because they are almost totally depleted. The depletion occurred because, all of a sudden, somebody found redfish were edible when blackened with Cajun spices. Before that, redfish were more of a scrap fish. But once somebody came up with a way of making a good dish out of them, the fishermen began taking them out by the tons. The redfish are almost totally gone now. Of course, everybody who's involved with fishing them is protesting the state bans because they want to harvest them to the last fish.

It's really a sad thing that humankind still seems to have a problem maintaining its balance with the creation. Many people are not ready to listen yet, even as the changes accelerate. But, on a personal level, I try to feel good because there's a growing number of people who *are* beginning to listen.

Sometime back, when I spoke in the Cincinnati area, I told people they should keep up to five gallons of water in containers in their houses because of the major changes that were coming and the major chemical disasters that would be happening. Some of those in the audience listened to me. A while later, in one area of Cincinnati, there was a major chemical spill and the water wasn't fit to drink. All of the bottled water was quickly gone from the stores. Those people who heard me and listened didn't go thirsty.

By the late 1980's there were at least 33 major cities in the United States where the water wasn't fit to drink. But people are drinking it because it's all they have. It's said that 93 percent of the water in the United States is polluted, and the same is true in Europe. Also, with drought in several parts of the world, water is becoming in short supply.

It's time we look at how we are living our lives. This is necessary for our survival as human beings. We can no longer wait until the future to do this. I want to stress again that 1973 was the beginning of the major change period for the Earth Mother. It was the beginning of the Earth cleansing. This period of time will go up to the year 2000. During this time major natural and human-caused disasters will be occurring. These disasters will be significant enough that people will have to agree there is something unusual happening.

Disasters are increasing in intensity to the point where they will be happening every day — somewhere. Every radio and television report that comes in tells us this is "a record cold . . . a record heat," a record this or that. This is part of the whole pattern. So are reports of destruction of the environmental balance. For example, one day newspapers report that frogs are becoming an endangered species in the western United States; the next day, zebra mussels are taking over most of the large lakes in the East.

The major changes began in 1973, but Native peoples in many parts of the world saw them coming. Sometimes we would try to warn people, such as in Bangladesh. There, holy men tried to warn the people that a great tidal wave was coming, but most didn't listen to them. They said the holy men were just trying to cook up some story to get them off their land so the holy men's followers could get on it. Ten days later, over 500,000 people lost their lives!

If a tornado strikes and wipes out a city or a major storm comes in, it's neither good nor evil. When a hurricane comes and rips up the coast, or other major changes occur in order for the Earth to survive, it's neither good nor evil. *It's just what is.*

Two Forks

There are two forks on the sacred tree that the Lakota people use in the Sun Dance. The forks represent the negative and the positive; we have both of these within us. How we respond to situations is within that fork. Dealing with "good" and "evil" is part of the processing the Creator put us here for. We might want to lay the blame on somebody else — like the Devil — but basically the Creator put us here to process our attitudes and come to our fullest level of consciousness and power. We are the ones who get to sort out whether we want to be goofy or do something worthwhile with our lives.

Understanding this idea is very important because so many of the Earth changes are caused by goofiness. For example, the intensity of hurricanes is going to increase greatly in the next several years because we have put so much carbon dioxide into the air. Many of the Earth changes are the result of cause and effect. If we cause something, whether through ignorance, arrogance or stupidity, we must live with the effect of our actions.

In the next ten to fifteen years, you're going to see such major changes at all levels that you won't recognize the world afterwards. Think about it. Between now and the year 2000 is the time span in which most of the major changes are going to be happening. They are happening right now, and they're going to intensify. It's not some little "maybe" thing anymore — it's for real and it's growing in strength.

The process for the Earth changes has been set in motion. One time I asked Spirit, "What about these powerful Earth changes that we see happening? Can events be changed? If tomorrow everybody was good and got down on their hands and knees and prayed, would that change it?"

"No, the changes are sealed," Spirit told me. "It's already happening." Then Spirit went further and supplied me with a little extra information that I didn't ask for. Spirit said, "You speak of 7.0 and 8.0 on your Richter scale for earthquakes. We speak of 10.0 and 12.0."

But there will be help. The powers and forces are here to help those people survive who are ready and willing to listen sincerely. They're here to help us right now; that is their purpose. In the same way, teachers like myself are here to help people during the time of the changes.

My people have a legend that says our teachers came down from the sky in a silver or white clamshell. When it settled onto the ground, the clamshell opened up and the teachers came out of it. This describes a spaceship perfectly. We have many records of such things among Native legends. I've had some very powerful experiences along this line also.

There are also spirit teachers among us already, people who carry the spirit power directly with them. They operate on a direct current basis with people they can contact. They've come here to do their work during this time. These teachers will be here through the year 2000 to help us through the Earth changes.

To me, the changes are not bad; they are very positive. But you need to be aware that these things are happening, are necessary, and that part of your role is to be aware and listening.

1987 was one of the most powerful years for humankind since the beginning of the Earth changes. It began a time of gathering loose ends together and collecting tremendous amounts of knowledge. The year 1987 started the period when individuals would have to open themselves up and accelerate their own ability to absorb and to learn.

Jade Eyes

The ancient Mayan temples have a specific number of steps. The Aztecs also used a certain number of steps in their temples. The steps represent a measurement of time. The last step on the temples is 1987 — it's the last date there. That is because the Mayan and Aztec prophets knew 1987 would be a time of major change in the world.

I saw some very powerful symbols that I was looking for at these temples. Back in 1980, when I went to New Zealand, my Maori brothers there told me that their history went back thousands of years. They told me they had traveled all over the Earth and done many ceremonial things. When I looked in the Mayan temple at Tecal, I saw the

Maori symbols; I knew that the story I had heard was true.

As I went along a sacred path near Tecal, I was praying. "Well, okay, Spirit," I prayed. "You're guiding me. Where do I step next? Where's the next rock to step on? Where do I go?"

I stayed on the path and found a mask-carver. When he carves a sacred mask, he prays for the spirit to go into it; and when he works with the sacred mask, he can become the power of that spirit. When I saw the mask he was carving, I recognized it immediately. The face of the mask had a beard and a little mustache, and crossed serpents and the quetzal birds of South America on it. Its features weren't Indian. This was the sacred mask of Quetzalcoatl, the great winged serpent. We're told that Quetzalcoatl returned in 1987 to bring back the teachings necessary for the next ten thousand years. The mask was meant for me.

Carrying this sacred mask has become a very powerful medicine. It's very interesting when I put it on. I see the world as if I were looking through jade eyes, as if the mask had sheets of green jade over it. Just as if I were looking through a pair of sunglasses, the world takes on a greenish hue.

In all the teachings I've had, I've always been told you have to prepare yourself before you put on a mask. When I pray and then put on that particular mask, I can call on the power represented by Quetzalcoatl. Then I'm able to transmit the power's knowledge. This is part of the Mayans' ancient teachings.

When I use the mask to work with dreams, I first pray with it, asking Spirit to help my dreams, to give me direction, to heal my dreams, to help me find my balance and to get rid of any negativity in my dreams so I can do my dream work clearly. The first night after I returned to the United States with this mask, I prayed with it, and then put it on before I went to sleep. Later that night I was down in Central America again. It was a very vivid dream: I was going to sacred places, sacred mountains, temples that haven't been uncovered yet. I was using copal incense to smudge there, and I started finding pieces of jade and certain ornaments. It was very powerful.

A really sad thing is the amount of knowledge that has been stolen from humanity. Down in the Mayan country, in the temples, there are rooms that once contained vast amounts of teachings in books made of bark. Now there is one manuscript left out of thousands, perhaps millions — the others were destroyed by the Spaniards. That one manuscript is the *Madrid Cortex*, which is now in Madrid, Spain. It is written in the Mayan language. In 1984, scientists "cracked" the Mayan alphabet. Now we Native people are harvesting as much of this knowledge as we can. We're working to bring all the ancient knowledge together again.

Love Life!

Many of you may have just come to a higher level of awareness in 1987. For you, it may seem like opening a book in the middle. Maybe you didn't get to read the first part of the book. But it happened whether you got a chance to read it or not. And it's happening! Just remember that.

The Earth changes are occurring in a very powerful manner. For your survival and the survival of your children, you're going to have to learn about them, and learn quickly. Spirit is watching people and trying to help them come into the next level of Earth consciousness — but something is being required of the people who are moving toward this knowledge.

If you want to survive the coming changes, remember this: the only people who are going to survive, Spirit says, are the people who are willing to make a conscious change in the way they look at life, in the way they understand things, and in their actions toward all creation. The people who survive will be those who love life and affirm life in every way they can.

Some very powerful things are going to happen during

the changes to show people how life really is. A lot of the things that people in power have tried to hide are going to be exposed. We've already seen quite a few hypocrisies revealed. Look at Mr. Reagan's deceptions, or at the preachers who were on television telling about how holy they were, while they were acting off-camera in ways they'd call sinful in others.

This exposure is necessary. People have to be shaken up and made aware that some of their leaders have been putting out a lot of nonsense for a long time. It's time to awaken people to true reality in a very strong way.

I have a spirit friend who travels with me now, and this friend has told me that I have to speak all the time. Even if I'm only speaking to one or two people, I have to at least say, "Hey, the Earth changes are happening."

I have some other "friends" that I'd like to take along when I travel, too, but people can't handle them at close range. I wear the emblem of one of them a lot of the time: the rattlesnake. But I don't take rattlesnake traveling because I find that people get nervous if a rattlesnake is curled up near me. People do understand the real power of rattlesnakes when they see them. What they need to learn is that the power of the changes is just as strong.

Up on Vision Mountain we see rattlesnakes now and then. If one gets too close to our home, we carefully carry the snake over to other parts of the mountain, especially when we're giving programs. Some people get upset when they see a rattlesnake curled up under a tree. But I love the snakes — I love them tremendously. I've made personal contact with them, so I feel really strong medicine from them.

When I go someplace, it is because people have invited me to come there. The Spirit tells me that the first thing I have to do is be invited. Otherwise, it's as though I am sticking my nose in other people's business. But when I am invited, then being there becomes a responsibility. After I give what I can, the responsibility shifts to those who invited me. If they want to continue the dance, their job is to keep in touch and to keep searching.

Everything Is Connected

In the period from 1929 to 1941, we went through what was called the Great Depression. During the Depression there was a tremendous weather change, a great drought cycle. This drought created the dust bowl and the winds blew the dust away, along with many people's dreams. People lost everything they had and went hungry.

Now, world leaders term the economic problems "recession" because "depression" frightens people too much. Anybody who survived the Depression knows there were major Earth disturbances during that time. It's also when Adolf Hitler came into power, when Joseph Stalin rose to power, and when World War II began.

Everything is interconnected. When Mt. St. Helens erupted in Washington State, there were riots in Miami. In Africa now, there is a severe drought. The deserts are growing every year, and there is much unrest on that continent, particularly in South Africa, but it is affecting other places, too. You see from these patterns that humankind and the Earth are very closely related. If something is strange or off balance in nature, people are affected by it.

Right now, you're seeing a lot of major Earth changes happening. You're also seeing very erratic behavior in human beings as a result. In the past decade there's been a very large number of suicides. In some cities across the United States, there are special squads that try to stop suicides. And more and more young people are committing suicide. What does it say about society when the young — those with most of their life ahead of them — kill themselves? And what can we do? Consider what happened recently on a reservation in Wyoming. Many young people were killing themselves. This suicide epidemic didn't stop until medicine people brought the sweat lodge and pipe ceremony to the young people.

A lot of families that have been together for years are breaking up. You're going to see more of this as the changes progress. Powerful things are happening; a lot of people are dying now because they can't handle it. I realize and acknowledge that there will be a lot of frightened people who will not survive. And some folks will leave just because they want to. That's all part of what will happen.

I'm worried about people who say that the Earth changes are taking place and there's nothing we can do about it. There are things you can do which I'll discuss more in Chapter Nine. But for now, let me just say you can start by storing food for yourself and loved ones. Just don't take on the attitude of the survivalist, because storing food alone will not save you. It's the change in thinking that will.

In reality, however, we're going to see a little bit of both attitudes. But the actual survivors won't be the people just sitting with their 30-06 rifles over a stash of canned pork & beans. The survivors will be the people who are also reaching out for another level of consciousness. The Bear Tribe, the group that I'm working with, is continuing to attract more of these kinds of people to our programs, as well as to our network in different places around the world. Through our work we're helping people through the time of the changes.

One way we help is by teaching people how to work with the Earth energy. When I am asked how I communicate with nature, I explain that I pray and feel a very strong connection — particularly with the thunder beings, the powers that direct the storms and the winds. When I pray to them, things happen. The spirit world doesn't speak English, or Chippewa, or German; it speaks its own language. The way the Earth knowledge comes to me is in a sensing, an inner feeling. This ability to sense, to feel, can be learned by most people.

Sometimes life gets very confusing to me. When that happens, I pray to the Creator for clarification. If nothing comes through, *I pray harder.* I pray, and I see things. A while back, I prayed during a drought cycle and I saw a map of the United States showing the drought area, as well as other areas that would be affected. Later that year, I saw the same map in *Newsweek* magazine. It is this way with many things. And that is why I believe very strongly in total communication with spirits and powers.

The ideas that I'm sharing with you do not constitute a philosophy of doom but one of hope. They show that there is going to be hope for the Earth Mother and for some human beings who live upon her.

What is really happening on Earth at this time is that consciousness is rising. That is the reason we are here: to share in this with all our brothers and sisters. In doing this, don't hide your knowledge or limit your consciousness; rather, bring your gifts forward.

Earth Tuning

The more I study other prophecies and teachings, the more I see the powerful parallels between them. I find our beginnings go much deeper than most people think. We're truly all related. Our common beginnings show us that at one time all people had a very strong connection with the creation around them. Our common ancestors were so strongly attuned to the Earth that they sensed everything about the Earth before it happened. That is a tuning that many Native peoples still retain.

Sometimes the Earth communication is garbled if you're just "listening" to newspapers, the radio or TV. I always feel very fortunate that I grew up in a quiet area in northern Minnesota. I feel happy that I grew up where I had 25 miles of back yard to play in. It gave me a sense of harmony with all creation. When you have a feeling of oneness with creation, you begin to have contact with both what is and what is to be. All of creation is intelligent — animals, plants, trees — and much more aware of what's happening and what's going to happen than most human beings. Most of our relations can sense things. Every so often the whales try to give us warnings. They try to let us know that something is off balance, and we've lost contact. But humans are arrogant, always referring to nature and the rest of creation around us as dumb. That is the reason we don't hear their communications. We've prejudiced ourselves against them. In so doing, we miss a lot of knowledge.

But I repeat: Before any major changes ever happen in the world, there are warnings. The creation and the powers around us transmit these cautions. For instance, trees broadcast warnings to each other before any major happening. Even *The New York Times*, of all places, reported that it has been established that trees communicate with each other. However, instead of looking at this as a way of opening up communication with trees, the scientists who made the discovery thought that with this knowledge they'd now be able to use pesticides and herbicides more effectively. That was all they got out of it.

It's really sad that we don't tune into the Earth. So many different times, when we have had the possibility of catching the bit of knowledge that might have pushed us forward and helped us tremendously, we didn't bother to reach. We didn't go for it. It's something to be aware of because there are many, many millions of people in the world who are dying or will die because of their prejudices, fears and their unwillingness to look at something new and open up to it.

It's Time

Sometimes I feel I am a stone age man stepping out into this big, busy technological world and telling people, "Hey, kids, it isn't going to work." Sometimes it frightens me a little bit because I tell people things and the next day they happen. Maybe I'm not the stone age man.

I was in Las Vegas when an earthquake hit Los Angeles — one of the big ones. The next day, as I flew in to Los

Angeles, I said to myself, "Well, that's over; I'll go in between them and come out again. Thank you, Great Spirit." That's just what happened. The day after I left, there was another good-sized quake.

Earth is a processing station, a place where we come to learn. All kinds of possibilities are open to us if we're ready to listen. And there are a lot of things we need to hear.

It's time now. We Native people have waited. We were told to stay quiet and wait. Some of us asked, "Well, should we go out and tell the other folks what they are doing to the Earth?" Spirit said, "No. Wait, wait." So we waited until we were told to go out and start teaching and sharing. Now that's what I am doing. It's very powerful to go out and share these things now because it's knowledge that's been here, just waiting to be shared.

When I first started speaking to people around 1970, my audiences were much smaller. Mostly they were long-haired people, hippies and such. Now the audiences are larger and a lot more varied. A lot of upper middle-class people are listening to what I say and really taking it seriously.

Awareness of the Earth changes is growing. The truth about them is in the papers daily now. Weather changes, natural disasters, more earthquakes, hungry and homeless people moving around the world — all these things are hard to ignore.

The 1990's will be hard because the changes will be accelerating. Major changes will come to some areas suddenly, and people will be without food, water, or gas for their cars. Some changes in one place will affect other areas, too. For instance, if major changes happen in southern California, a lot of people across the country will be without many fresh foods.

In Mexico City during the time of their big 1985 earthquake, the water supply was disrupted, food became scarce, and people couldn't get in or out. During the October 1989 San Francisco earthquake, similar things happened. These were quakes affecting just one city. When you multiply that by multi-city quakes, then you know there will be even more problems.

I know it is a hard thing to realize, but the changes — the Great Purification as many Native people call it — are necessary. If the corrections which will result from them aren't made, then those people who don't have a sense of balance could succeed in destroying the Earth, probably contaminating it beyond any chance of recovery. I see the Earth changes as positive because they are necessary for the survival of the planet. If humanity is going to survive these changes, we will have to develop a much higher consciousness. Such a change will be very positive and good for all of creation.

Often I am asked if the Earth changes can be prevented. I don't feel the Earth will be eased any by forgetting the past. As I've said, when I asked Spirit this question, I was told, "No, it is sealed, it has already happened."

What people can do is prepare, reach out to each other and start to find a better balance in their lives. The Earth changes are here now and will continue for some time. It's not the end of the world for everyone or the planet. It's the beginning of a new age for those willing to change themselves. Those people who survive the changes, who live through them, will be those who have prepared for them on all levels of their lives. *Black Dawn/Bright Day* is a handbook for that preparation.

Chapter Four

The Sad Statistics

When I used to talk with people about the Earth changes, even as recently as 1986, I would tell about one bad drought, or one large earthquake, or one severe chemical disaster, and that would sum up what was happening with those kinds of Earth changes. Now things are occurring so rapidly, I have to update my examples weekly, even daily. You don't have to be a true believer to know about the changes. All you have to do is follow the news.

To give you some idea of the reality of the Earth changes and what you can expect in the future, I'm going to tell you in this chapter about some of the more dramatic changes that had occurred on the planet by the Spring Equinox of 1990. Unfortunately, some of these statistics will be outdated before this book even gets into print — replaced by ones that are worse. I hope that reading all these statistics in one chapter will give you a good idea of the seriousness and the immensity of the problems we now face.

This chapter will not be easy reading. Believe me, it wasn't easy writing. Some of the facts here will be familiar. Some may seem strange and new. I realize that statistics can be presented in many ways; playing with numbers is a game this society likes. Taking that into consideration, I feel the important thing here is to look at these facts and numbers all together because they clearly show what kind of a tapestry the dominant society has woven upon the Earth Mother. This will help you to understand the need for the changes that are here now. If you don't want to be like an ostrich, constantly presenting your hind end to the world, it is necessary to pull your head up out of the sand sometimes, even if the light feels unpleasant.

I've begun this chapter with a short overview of some ecological problems that occur around the world in a minute, an hour, and a day. Following that, I present a closer look at some of the problem areas.

Overview

A Canadian-based environmental group called Global Awareness in Action has gleaned the following statistics from a variety of scientific and governmental sources. What they report is consistent with what I've learned from numerous sources, and what I'll teach you in the following sections.

Each Minute

- At least 51 acres of tropical forests are destroyed.
- We consume almost 35,000 barrels of oil.
- 50 tons of fertile soil are washed or blown off cropland.
- We add 12,000 tons of carbon dioxide to the atmosphere.

Each Hour

- 1,692 acres of productive dry land become desert.
- 1,800 children die of malnutrition and hunger (that makes a total of 15 million each year).
- 120 million dollars are spent for military expenditures (making a total of one trillion each year).
- 55 people are poisoned by the pesticides they use; 5 die.
- 60 new cases of cancer are diagnosed in the United States alone (that makes a total of 500,000 each year with 20,000 leading to death).

Each Day

- Over 230,000 babies are born.
- 25,000 people die of water shortage or contamination.
- 10 tons of nuclear waste are generated by the 350 existing nuclear plants.
- 250,000 tons of sulfuric acid fall as acid rain in the Northern Hemisphere.
- 60 tons of plastic packaging and 372 tons of fishing net are dumped into the sea by commercial fishermen.
- Almost 5 species of life become extinct.

according to an economic forecasting firm.

Carbon dioxide is now known to cause only half the problem of the greenhouse effect. The rest comes from other gases. Chlorofluorocarbons, nitrous oxides (from auto exhaust and power plants), and methane (from natural gas, rotting garbage, bacteria in cattle and termites, and the muck of rice paddies) are other major contributors to the greenhouse effect.

Weather conditions now seem to foreshadow the greenhouse effect. In 1988 sections of the Midwestern and Great Plains areas of the United States had drier conditions than in the past 87 years. The drought broke in most of the country in 1989, but severe problems persisted in pockets of these important agricultural areas. By the Spring Equinox of 1990, some parts of these areas still suffered dustbowl conditions.

In the Midwestern and Western parts of the United States, many cattlemen have been reducing their herds because dry rangeland just cannot support the animals.

To see the extent of what is happening with the weather, let's look at some of the worst disasters caused by climate changes in a five-month period of 1988-89. These statistics come from the magazine *Pulse of the Planet*.*

- November, 1988 — 1,000 dead, many missing as the result of a tropical cyclone causing floods and tidal waves in Bangladesh and East India.
- December, 1988 — freak winds in Southern California topple a radio tower and sink boats.
- December, 1988 — floods kill 53 people on Java in Indonesia.
- December, 1988 — freak rains and snowstorms in the Middle East.
- January, 1989 — unusually cold conditions in the Southwestern United States; a rare cold wave in Northern

* The journal of the Orgone Biophysical Research Laboratory, PO Box 1395, El Cerrito, CA 94530. Write them for subscription information.

India and the Philippines.
- January, 1989 — mysterious dark rain falls in Kenya during thunderstorms.
- January, 1989 — a week of rain in Indonesia leaves 27 dead and 12,000 homeless.
- February, 1989 — heavy monsoon rains and floods leave 120 dead in the Philippines; an Arctic cold blast hits the North Central United States with winds over 100 miles per hour in Montana.
- February, 1989 — rare snowfalls in the Southwestern United States and in the Canary Islands.
- February, 1989 — freak hurricane force winds in Ireland and Northern Britain; second major snowstorms in Jordan and Lebanon; heavy rains and snow in the Midwestern and Eastern United States and Indonesia.
- February, 1989 — floods in Peru and the Eastern United States; 12 weeks of dry conditions in Europe and the Middle East.
- March, 1989 — abnormally high ocean temperatures near the Philippines; floods in Southern Africa leaving 100 dead and 50,000 homeless; wildfires in Brazil and Florida.

According to a report in the Woodrew Update from Canada, Cliff Harris, one of Canada's leading climatologists, said in 1988 that "things, weatherwise, are becoming increasingly berserk on a global basis. The current worldwide cycle of topsy-turvy temperatures and record breaking storms will get a lot worse before things begin to improve after the year 2005."

Harris further predicted that the years between 1992-96 will be the most extreme in terms of weather in 510 years. Among other things, he expects a record drought in the 1990's.

Try making your own record of the weather in your area for a month or longer, and use this record to prove the existence of weather changes to yourself.

Seismic Events

From the planet's beginnings about 4.5 billion years ago, there have been continuous shifts in the shape it has taken. In the past, large shifts in Earth's topology or climate have been accompanied by waves of extinctions. The most spectacular example is the dying off of the dinosaurs 65 to 136 million years ago.

During this present time of Earth change, increased seismic activity is taking place. And the earthquakes are getting larger. From 1950 to 1990, the number of large earthquakes — 6.0 or greater on the Richter scale — almost doubled compared to the first 50 years of this century.

Since 1970, twenty-four "killer earthquakes" — 1,000 or more dead — have struck. On May 31, 1970, an earthquake with a magnitude of 7.7 hit Chimbote, Peru, killing 68,000 people. On February 4, 1976, Guatemala City suffered a 7.5 earthquake that killed 23,000. On July 28, 1976, Tangshan, China, was hit by an 8.2 quake which killed 800,000. Tabas, Iran, had a 7.7 quake on September 16, 1978, which killed 25,000. In 1985 Mexico City suffered a 7.9 quake which killed 10,000. Armenia in the Soviet Union was hit by a major quake on December 7, 1988, which killed 60,000 people. As this book was being written, in June 1990, a 7.7 earthquake hit Iran, killing over 50,000 people.

In July 1989, Oshima, Japan, was jolted by 2,500 Earth tremors in a seven-day period.

On October 17, 1989, an earthquake measuring 6.9 on the Richter scale rocked the San Francisco area killing over 100 people and causing millions of dollars in damage to an area that extended from the quake's epicenter, 65 miles south of San Francisco, to the northern part of San Francisco. The quake caused large fires from broken gas lines and severe damage to some of the bridges linking parts of the area. It also caused many Californians to think about "The Big One" — the large earthquake scientists expect to hit that part of the Earth in the foreseeable future.

To get some idea of the constancy of Earth movement

today, following are the movements that occurred in a time period of a little over three months (November 25, 1988, to March 1, 1989). Again, I am relying upon the *Pulse of the Planet* magazine for this list of earthquakes of 6.0 or more on the Richter scale:

- Canada — November 25th (strongest in 56 years)
- South China — November 30th (more than 500 homes destroyed)
- Tonga Islands — December 5th
- Armenia, USSR — December 7th (60,000 killed, massive and widespread damage)
- Carmadek Islands — December 16th
- The Soviet Union — December 21st
- Tonga Islands — January 2nd
- Kuril Islands — January 9th
- Seram, Asia — January 10th
- New Britain Islands — January 17th
- Mid-Indian Rise — January 20th (two in one day)
- Japan — January 22nd
- Tadzhik, USSR — January 22nd (only 5.5 on the Richter scale but killed 1,000 people and caused extensive mud-slides)
- Comondroski Islands — January 27th
- New Ireland — February 4th
- Molucca Passage — February 10th
- Northeastern Indonesia — February 13th
- Solomon Islands — February 14th
- Easter Islands — February 16th
- Carmadek Islands — February 25th
- Northeastern Indonesia — February 27th
- Kuril Islands — March 1st

During this same time period, Mount Tokachi in Japan erupted on December 19, 1988, after being dormant for 26 years. Lonquimay Volcano in Chile erupted on December 28th for the first time in 100 years, while Mount Tokachi had its second and third eruptions. Mount Tutupaca in Peru, dormant for 100 years, began issuing smoke and gas in January 1989, while eruptions continued from Mount Lonquimay in Chile. Later in January, Mounts Llaima, Tolhuece and Villarrica in Chile awoke while Mount Lonquimay spewed a three-mile lava flow, and Mount Tokachi erupted again.

In December 1989, Redoubt Volcano near Anchorage, Alaska, erupted sending ash and steam eight miles into the air. It had major eruptions again in January and March, 1990.

Population

By the year 1800, there were one billion people living on Earth. That number doubled by 1930, and doubled again by 1975. If the current birthrate stays as it is, the world's present population of 5.1 billion will double again by the year 2029. Ninety percent of that growth will be in developing countries, with African nations expanding at the fastest rate. By 2020 the population of Kenya, at its current 4 percent growth rate, will jump from 23 million to 274 million. The growth rate in Brazil, China, India and Indonesia is lower but the number of people in these countries means a huge increase in people nonetheless.

It is estimated that 60 million people will starve to death in 1990. Each day in developing countries, according to TIME magazine, 40,000 babies die of starvation.

Mexico City was described by TIME as "struck by a population bomb." It is the fastest growing urban center on Earth. In 1989, it had 20 million residents, up from 9 million only 20 years before. Some people consider this city — plagued by overpopulation, severe pollution, and grinding poverty — a forerunner for other urban areas.

In India, according to government reports, 37 percent of the people cannot buy enough food to sustain themselves. Some officials fear that constant hunger could create groups of people without enough physical energy to help themselves in any way.

Environmentalists have urged the world to adopt the

goal of cutting the Earth's population growth-rate in half during the 1990's. That would mean a two-child family, at most, for the world as a whole. Today, virtually all Third World countries are committed to limiting population growth.

According to surveys by the United Nations and other organizations, fully half the 483 million married women in developing countries (except China) do not want more children. Yet they have little or no access to effective birth control methods.

The Bangladesh government began in 1975 to upgrade the social and economic status of women in some areas; 75 percent of the women of childbearing age living in those areas now use contraceptives, while only 35 percent do in other parts of the country.

The World Bank estimates that making birth control readily available would require that the current $3 billion expenditure for family planning be increased to $8 billion by the year 2000. That expenditure could mean that in the next 60 years world population would be 8 billion rather that 10 billion.

Water

The Sierra Club reported in 1989 that toxic contamination of the Great Lakes is worsening despite massive cleanup efforts by the United States and Canada. Research indicates that this is because airborne pollution, which kills wildlife, causes deformities in waterfowl (10 to 40 times greater in the birds of the Great Lakes than in those from other regions), and endangers human health is carried by prevailing wind patterns from as far away as Central America.

Some scientists say that even if all polluting were stopped immediately, it would take 100 years to get rid of the traces of pollutants already in the Great Lakes. Because of the contaminants in the water of these lakes, anyone eating fish from them is also consuming the contaminants.

In 1980, four out of five child deaths in the Third World

were caused by disease from dirty water supplies. Eighty percent of the people in developing countries have no sanitation facilities. Water shortage and contamination kill 25,000 people a day. More than two thirds of India's waters are polluted; 98 percent of China's sewage goes into rivers untreated. Yet a ten-year international plan to supply clean water in the developing world would take no more than what is now spent in ten days for global military expenditures.

In the late 1980's, fishermen off Rhode Island reported that the lobster catch from canyons along the continental shelf had dropped 70 percent in a little over a year. Catches of other fish reportedly dropped at least 50 percent. Fishermen said this was happening because some New York and New Jersey municipalities had begun dumping their sewer sludge in an area where the water currents carry it to these shelf canyons.

At any one time, 33 percent of all the United States shellfishing beds are closed due to pollution contamination, according to the publication WORLD WATCH.

One year in the late 1980's, over 200 dead porpoises washed ashore along the Atlantic. Needles, syringes and hospital wastes kept washing up on the beaches of New Jersey and Long Island.

In the Albermarle-Pamlico Sound, off North Carolina, the situation reflects what is occurring in other parts of the Atlantic Ocean, as well as in other waters of the world: fungal diseases are eating into the shells of shellfish and causing sores in the sides of fish; brown tides — a bloom of toxic algae — have also been found here, forcing the closing of parts of the shoreline's top fishing. Indigenous, non-toxic algae so deoxygenated the water that eels, crabs, and even fish were crawling onto the banks because they could not breath in the water.

The Environmental Defense Fund has found that acid rain is doing direct damage to coastal waters. The nitrogen compounds involved in acid rain are key nutrients leading to the algae blooms that deoxygenate water and kill everything in it.

The algae bloom or red tide phenomenon is on the rise globally and has killed fish in areas as large as 400 square miles. Japan's Inland Sea has up to 200 red tides annually. Algae blooms in the North Sea have recently increased by 400 percent. One bloom in an area that connects the North Sea and the Baltic Sea killed all marine life to a depth of 50 feet. (Almost 50 percent of the Baltic Sea's bottom waters are already oxygen-less.)

At least six major red tides have occurred along the East Coast of the United States since 1972, in regions where they were once rare. One form of algae, heretofore common only in the Gulf of Mexico, recently struck beaches near Cape Hatteras, North Carolina, causing a $25 million loss to the area's fishing and tourism industries; 3,000 dolphins were killed.

A dead zone, one with virtually no oxygen, 300 miles long and 10 miles wide, was adrift in the Gulf of Mexico in 1988.

Agriculture

Almost a quarter of the world's land surface — approximately 7.5 billion acres — is at risk from desertification, salinization from bad irrigation, or other degradation.

According to the World Resources Institute and the International Institute for Environment and Development, more than 60 percent of the world's productive drylands have suffered losses of biological productivity, which may lead to desert-like conditions. They report, in addition, that by the year 2000 the urban population of developing regions will be twice the size of the urban population in the developed world. Half the Earth's population will live in urban areas — generators of sewage, trash and industrial waste.

According to Worldwatch Institute, in 1988 the United States became a "food deficit" nation. It produced 196

80

million tons of grain and consumed 206 million. The more than 100 nations that purchase food from the United States were being supplied by reserves, which in 1989 were down to one third of what they were in 1987, as the result of the severe drought of 1988.

The power over America's food supply is concentrated in fewer and fewer hands. Four multinational corporations control over 85 percent of the United States grain market. Farmers make up less than 2 percent of the United States population, yet produce enough food to feed all of its people and provide more than 85 percent of the world's surplus. But farmers are becoming more dependent on energy-consuming technology and getting less back from the land because of soil erosion due to poor farming practices. By 1990, 75 percent of the original topsoil found in the United States when the Europeans first arrived had been lost. The soil is also being worn out through chemical use.

Overgrazing and overcropping, which cause the topsoil to erode, are serious problems in 43 countries. Heavy losses of forests have occurred in at least 24 developing countries.

Every day in the United States, 12 square miles of prime farmland are lost to developers. According to the American Farmland Trust, that means more than three million acres of productive land are consumed each year by urbanization.

One of five pesticides exported from the United States to developing countries has been banned in the United States. 490,000 pesticide poisoning cases occur in the world annually. One in ten ends in death.

Between 1970 and 1980, the number of insects and mites resistant to key pesticides increased seventeenfold due to overuse of these chemicals. Yet, up to 64 percent of the pesticides applied to wheat, for instance, may end up, unaltered, in bread.

Garbage

Each year, Americans throw away 16 billion disposable diapers, 1.5 billion pens, 220 million tires, and 2 billion razors and blades. Yearly, Americans discard enough aluminum to rebuild the entire United States commercial airline fleet every three months.

In the United States, 80 percent of solid waste is now dumped in 6,000 landfills. From 1985 to 1990, 3,000 dumps were closed. By the year 1993, 2,000 more will be filled and closed.

By 1990, Japan recycled 50 percent of its trash, Western Europe around 30 percent and the United States only 10 percent.

Toxic Waste

In 1989, the Environmental Protection Agency announced that American industry poured more than 22 billion pounds of toxic chemicals into the air, water and land in one year (1987). Of these, 9.7 billion pounds went into streams and other bodies of water; 2.7 billion pounds went into landfills; 3.2 billion pounds were injected deep into the ground; 1.9 billion pounds were shipped to municipal waste water treatment plants; and 2.6 billion pounds were sent to off-site treatment and disposal facilities. These toxic substances consist of more than 300 chemicals, including an assortment known to cause cancer and other serious illnesses. Texas had the most pollutants overall. These are the statistics with only 75 percent of the companies required to report doing so.

Oil spills became increasingly common in the late 1980's and early 1990's. The most devastating one of that period was the oil spill of the Exxon tanker *Valdez* in the Prince William Sound off the south coast of Alaska. The spill was of almost 11 million gallons. It contaminated at least 1,090 miles of shoreline, killing immediately at least 33,000 birds, 980 otters, 138 eagles and untold numbers of fish and other marine wildlife. Up to 1,600 dead birds showed up on nearby Kodiak Island in the months after, and the full consequence of the spill will not be known for years to come. It took 12,000 people and at least $1.28 billion to clean up some of the disaster and recover 2.6 million gallons of oil.

The United States National Research Council says that 21 million barrels of oil enter the sea each year from small but steady sources worldwide. This is in addition to the 600,000 barrels that are accidentally spilled each year. According to Worldwatch Institute, as little as one part of oil per ten million parts of seawater has *serious* effects upon plankton and other marine life. The Indian Ocean is reported to be the most polluted by oil.

Nuclear

Norwegian scientists at the State Institute for Radiation Hygiene said in 1990 that radiation from the 1986 Soviet nuclear disaster at Chernobyl is lingering in their country ten times longer than predicted. It warned Norwegians to be wary about eating untested meat and fish. Some meat and fish were higher in radiation in 1988-89 than in 1986, presumably because radiation built up in some plants that were eaten by livestock. All the reindeer herds of the Laplanders had to be destroyed because of radiation from Chernobyl.

Radioactive nuclear fuel waste totaled 6,219 tons in 1970. By 1985, it had grown to over 59,000 tons. Reprocessing plutonium, the only way to produce suitable radioactive material for nuclear weapons, increases the total volume of radioactive waste by 150 times.

To date, no suitable method for long-term storage of nuclear waste has been developed anywhere in the world. In the United States, no permanent repository has been sited; the majority of radioactive waste is housed in "temporary" containers, even though most of it will remain lethal for thousands of years.

Accumulated radioactivity dumped into the Atlantic

totals over one million curies. Plutonium dumped into the North Sea from 1960 to 1990 was enough to give cancer to 250 million people. After 100,000 years it would still be lethal to 15.5 million people.

In the late 1980's, it was revealed that federal weapons-making plants had secretly littered large areas of the United States with radioactive waste. The United States government also admitted to deliberately exposing residents of south-central Washington State to large doses of radiation during two planned releases 40 years ago.

Between 1949 and 1989, a total of more than 1,800 nuclear bomb tests took place in the Soviet Union, the South Pacific, China, the United States and in other secret locations.

Over 680 of these bomb tests were held at the Nevada Nuclear Test Site, most of which were above ground until 1963. Over 3,000 acres of the Nevada Nuclear Test Site are now contaminated with radioactive or other hazardous wastes, according to the *San Francisco Chronicle*.

In the first 50 years of this century, there were on average 68 earthquakes a year of 6.0 or higher on the Richter scale. Since 1950, the average number of such large earthquakes has almost doubled, to 127 a year. According to Dr. Gary T. Whiteford at the University of New Brunswick in Canada, this huge increase in large earthquakes since 1950 is the result of atomic bomb testing, which began in earnest that year.

Dr. Yoshio Kato of Tokai University in Japan has also found a strong correlation between atomic bomb testing and large earthquakes. Research at Tokai University further shows abnormal wandering of the Earth's magnetic polar movement and an increase in exospheric temperature of up to 150 degrees centigrade following atomic bomb tests.

Acid Rain
Ninety percent of the sulphur present in the skies over

Europe and North America by the late 1980's came not from natural causes but from the burning of coal and oil. Sulphur is a key cause of acid rain.

In the northeastern United States, rain can be 100,000 to 1 million times as acid as tap water, and 10,000 times as acid as normal rain.

In Scotland, rain can be as acid as vinegar; snow has been reported turned black by power station emissions in that country.

Acid rain has reportedly eliminated trout in many rivers in Norway; acidified 90,000 kilometers of brooks and 18,000 lakes in Sweden; and severely affected over 50 lochs in Scotland, 700,000 lakes in Canada, and thousands more in the United States.

In West Germany, the percentage of trees damaged by acid rain rose from 35 percent to 50 percent between 1983 and 1984.

Forests

Tropical forests cover only 7 percent of the surface of the Earth, but they provide habitat for between 50 and 80 percent of the planet's species.

Only 1.7 million of the estimated 5 to 30 million different life forms on the Earth have been catalogued. It is likely that by the year 2000 hundreds of thousands of unknown species will be extinct because of the current destruction of tropical forests. Less than 5 percent of the world's tropical forests receive any protection against damage or destruction.

Over the past 100 years, half of what was 7.7 million square miles of rain forest has vanished. The problem began in Africa where the colonial nations allowed private companies to harvest timber without any restrictions. When the African people gained independence, they often continued to sell the timber because it was one of their most profitable products.

Worldwide, at least 40 percent of the rain forests were

lost between 1960 and 1990. For every 25 acres of trees that have been felled, an average of less than one tree has been planted.

The World-Wide Fund for Nature estimates that at least 77,000 square miles of tropical forests fall to the saw and the flames every year. The United Nations Development Program says that only a nuclear war could equal the global effects of the destruction of the tropical forests.

In Third World countries, at least 27 million acres of forest — an area as big as Tennessee — are either slashed and burned or flooded for dams each year. The most alarming destruction is in the Amazon Basin. (Not coincidentally, the indigenous people of the Amazon region have gone from numbering three million in the early part of this century to a population of 250,000 in 1989.)

According to Brazil's Space Studies Institute, which conducts satellite surveys, fires set in 1987 to clear the Amazon for farmers and ranchers destroyed 80,000 square miles of rain forest. In 1988, 50,000 square miles of forest lands were burned, of which 30 to 40 percent were virgin rain forest.

The environmental disaster in the Amazon is exacerbated by recent installations of giant power plants, mines and factories. To operate, these all require wood.

Coca growers also chop down large stretches of Amazon rain forest and dump millions of gallons of toxic chemicals into the Amazon River. Coca growers, who produce 75 percent of the primary source of cocaine consumed in the United States, have invaded two national parks and two national forests. They use fertilizers, pesticides and herbicides, including Agent Orange and paraquat, to clear land and to care for their crop.

Some side effects of the Amazonian deforestation that contribute to other ecological problems come from the fires used to rid the area of trees. In 1989, these fires in Brazil produced approximately 600 million tons of carbon dioxide, 44 million tons of carbon monoxide, 6 million tons of particulate, 5 million tons of methane, 2.5 million tons of ozone, and more than one million tons of nitrogen oxides, according to the *Earth Island Journal.*

To preserve the rain forests, the developed nations must make it as profitable to the developing nations to keep the forests, as it now is to allow their destruction. The total sum the United Nations estimates is needed for tropical reforestation and conservation is equal to half a day's expenditure on military armaments worldwide. (Implementing a world plan to combat desertification would take two days' expenditure on arms.)

According to columnist Tom Wicker, an area of China the size of Italy (about 129,000 square miles) has been denuded of forests and has become a virtual desert in the last 30 years; that in turn caused floods, drought and food shortages. China has since undertaken the world's largest reforestation project.

Deserts are growing worldwide with about 70,000 square kilometers of additional desert land appearing each year. Deforestation is a major cause. Half of the world's population relies on noncommercial firewood as its sole energy source, which contributes heavily to the desertification of the planet.

The United States settlers deforested most of the continent as they moved westward. Only on the Pacific Slope are old-growth forests in sizable tracts still found. With current lumber practices, they could be gone in 20 to 30 years. Every eight seconds, an acre of trees in the United States disappears.

The American Forestry Association has identified 20 million open acres in the Southeast alone that should be planted in trees. In the "heat islands" of cities, towns and suburbs, the Association cites a need for 100 million more trees planted around houses and businesses and 60 million more along streets by 1992 to achieve a significant energy saving.

One Connecticut utility announced in 1988 that it would

plant 52 million trees in Guatemala. That was the number necessary to compensate for emissions from its new 180-megawatt coal-burning power plant.

Endangered Species

According to an article in the *Washington Post*, Lake Victoria, the greatest freshwater lake in Africa, may be on the brink of an ecological collapse that would rob millions of lakeshore people of their major source of protein. This lake, the third largest in the world, is now inhabited by only three species of fish when once it contained hundreds of species. One of the dominant species is the Nile perch, a carnivore that can grow to six feet and weigh several hundred pounds. The Nile perch was introduced by British colonists in the 1960's with the idea of attracting tourists through sport fishing. What these people failed to consider was that the perch would eat a lot of the native fish that provided food to the eight million Africans who live along the shoreline in Kenya, Tanzania and Uganda.

A combination of the Nile perch and other environmental problems, such as deforestation and acid rain, have severely affected Lake Victoria's ecosystem to the point where scientists estimate that the bottom third of the lake is now anaerobic, a dead zone where no fish can survive due to the lack of oxygen.

In 1981, the official endangered species list worldwide stood at 230. By 1989, it numbered 35,000. One quarter or more of the Earth's species of animals, plants, microbes and fungi will become extinct unless measures are taken to preserve them, according to the National Science Foundation.

According to World Resources, in Southeast Asia, 68 percent of the wildlife habitat has disappeared; in sub-Sahara Africa, 65 percent has disappeared.

From 1979 through 1989, the African elephant went from a total population of 1.3 million to little more than 600,000 — a kill rate that, if continued, will destroy the species in another ten years.

In 1989, scientists working with the International Whaling Commission announced that the blue whale, the largest animal ever to live on Earth, is a lot closer to extinction than previously believed. In a decade-long survey off Antarctica, they found only 453 whales in an area where they had expected to find ten times that many.

By the year 2050, one in four of all plant species alive today is expected to be extinct. There are no laws protecting plants, so landowners may pluck or bulldoze the last specimen of the rarest plant on Earth without suffering any consequences. According to the Nature Conservancy in Florida, the federal government lists only 27 plants for protection and these are protected only if they are on land that somehow receives federal funds. Some plant species being destroyed are so new they have yet to be given Latin names.

Wilderness

According to two environmental geographers using maps from the United States Defense Mapping Agency, in the late 1980's the following portions of land areas were without traces of human habitation:

- Antarctica — 100% wilderness
- North America — 37.5% wilderness
- Soviet Union — 33.6% wilderness
- Australia & South Pacific — 27.9% wilderness
- Africa — 27.5% wilderness
- South America — 20.8% wilderness
- Asia — 13.6% wilderness
- Europe — 2.8% wilderness

Only 20 percent of this wilderness land is protected from exploitation, with about half in danger of immediate exploitation. A large percentage of this land is uninhabitable desert, mountain or scrubland.

The Ozone Layer

The stratospheric ozone layer soaks up the sun's ultraviolet rays and prevents lethal levels of solar radiation from reaching the ground. The ozone is damaged or destroyed by chlorofluorocarbons (CFC's), which are used in air conditioning systems, plastic foam cartons, some aerosols, dry cleaning solvents and industrial production. Once released, CFC's can take 15 years to reach the ozone layer. The ozone depletion that has already occurred will result in more deaths from skin cancer, more vulnerability to infectious diseases, cell and tissue damage in plants and damage to ocean plankton. It would take an 85-percent cut in CFC use today just to keep stratospheric concentrations at today's levels in the next two decades.

In 1988, a three-percent thinning of the stratospheric ozone layer over Europe was detected. A "hole" the size of the United States developed in the ozone layer over the Antarctic in the late 1980's.

The depleted ozone layer and increased "hard" ultraviolet radiation that comes with it could have a disastrous effect on marine phytoplankton — the microscopic plants that live in the surface layer of the oceans. Phytoplankton, the building block of the marine food chain, produce approximately 40 percent of the Earth's oxygen. According to researchers from Texas A&M University, working in Antarctica where the ozone depletion is most serious, increases in ultraviolet radiation decrease photosynthesis in the phytoplankton. It has also been estimated that at about 16 percent depletion of the stratospheric ozone layer, phytoplankton in the oceans will die-off spontaneously.

Chapter Five

The
Death Culture

To me, the Earth is a living, intelligent being. I made the analogy earlier that the Earth is like a great big shaggy dog, and we humans are acting like fleas in its hair. And when that shaggy dog gets annoyed and starts scratching and shaking, all of the little fleas get very frightened. Well, there is going to be a lot of shaking and a lot of frightened humans during the Earth changes.

Humans have to realize they are just another species on the planet, like the deer or the sage — except that when humans over-populate, they threaten the life of the planet because of the way they use, and misuse, the resources. Five billion people on the planet as of 1990 represents a pretty heavy burden. It wouldn't be so hard on the planet if people learned to walk lightly, but they haven't.

We have a responsibility to the Earth to come back into harmony and balance. We must become the protectors and keepers of the Earth again. We have to learn what the Native people have learned — walk in a sacred manner upon the Earth. This means, wherever we walk and move upon the Earth, we acknowledge that this planet is a living, intelligent being. We have to treat it with love and respect. We cannot go on polluting and destroying the planet, creating more ecological disasters every year. The fact that we do is exactly why the planet can't handle it anymore. The disasters we continue to create explain why the Earth is responding in what seems like an unfriendly manner toward humans at this time.

The dominant society's approach to the Earth is that of a "Death Culture." For instance, people cut down all the trees around a pond in the mountains. Then the pond dries up and there is no water for the animals. The watershed is gone because, without the trees, the snows don't stay. So the mountain becomes barren. And for every large tree which is cut down it takes approximately 2,500 seedlings to replace its oxygen output. So we lose that oxygen. If we keep it up, humans will be a dead culture. If we would only realize that it takes twelve trees to provide enough oxygen for each one of us, we might look differently at them, and at the magnitude of the other things we are doing to the planet and all our relations upon it.

Many years back I was telling people that the time was coming when one area would be too wet, another too dry; one place too hot, another too cold. For a long time I've been telling people the Earth Mother would withhold her increase. From the preceding chapter, it should be clear that these climate shifts are occurring right now. This is exactly what is happening. And it is happening so quickly that each day brings new stories of weather disturbances, abnormalities, seismic activity, and human-caused imbalances in the ecosystem, which in turn create economic and political consequences.

In "The Sad Statistics," I gave you an overview of the worldwide problems we now face. In this chapter I'm going to give you a close-up view of some specific problems before I go into the underlying causes of all our global troubles in the next chapter. But first, let's look at some of the stories of the death culture, and consider the connections between humans and the Earth.

In 1988 there was a major drought in the United States, while in Germany there was so much rain they didn't know what to do with it. The next year there was too much rain on the East coast of the United States, while the Midwest, West, and Southwest experienced moderate to severe drought. In 1989, much of the United States was in a drought and flood cycle. In fact, some drought areas saw their lowest amount of moisture in 1989. The Mississippi/Missouri river system was the driest it had ever been in recorded history. The Army Corps of Engineers had to deepen the channel of the Mississippi River in order to keep the boats floating.

In Africa, an area the size of Massachusetts becomes desert every year. This is added on to the desert already there. At one time the African people farmed land that is now desert and used the same pastures for their goats for thousands of years. Then, as I mentioned earlier, the governments of some of the technologically-advanced countries wanted to sell a lot of farm machinery. So they said to the African governments, "We'll show you how to really farm. We'll show you how to get really high-profit crops off this land." The African governments agreed. Then men came in with bulldozers and tractors and tore up the thin topsoil — the two or three inches of fragile topsoil that is the African land.

This kind of farming gave the Africans two or three years of good crops. They called this period the "Green Revolution." But then the people discovered the topsoil was gone, and so was their ability to farm. Now you find areas where the Africans sold off their timber because they didn't have anything else to sell or any other way to eat. They *had* to sell their trees. You can go out into the desert there and see the stumps of great trees that were cut down and sold. Losing the trees created more desert and less acreage for crops, which resulted in decreased food supplies and, eventually, the horrible famines on that continent.

They say in another 50 years all of Africa will be desert. Desert begets desert. Desert begets drought. Through the misuse and abuse of resources there, many areas are drying up completely.

You need to be aware of what is happening all around the world because this is our common Earth Mother. In the 1980's in Brazil, at least 5,000 acres of trees were being cut down every day. The trees were just cut down and burned so big businesses could farm the land or raise cattle to make hamburgers for the fast food restaurants in the industrialized nations. Because people in developed countries eat junk food, many South American people starve. And every year more of the rain forest is being destroyed.

There are at least five species — plant, animal or insect — that become extinct every day. They *no longer exist* in the world. Many people don't notice their disappearance until there are only three hundred of a species left. Then all of a sudden there's the last one, and then they're all gone. In my lifetime, I've seen many types of ducks and other creatures disappear from the face of the Earth. This is happening in Latin America, the United States, Europe, all over the world. And much of it is so stupid. In Peru, merchants sell collections of Amazon butterflies cheaply. And they'll keep doing it until there are almost no butterflies left in the wild. Then they'll collect the remaining few for "Butterfly Houses" like they have in Europe.

What Is Happening With The Weather?

Over a decade ago Spirit told me to tell people that we're moving into a time of major Earth changes, a time when the Earth Mother will withhold her increase. I've seen this in my dreams, and it is part of Indian prophecies also. Major weather patterns will be changing very rapidly and, as a result, we will have to pray very hard for our crops during these times just so we can stay alive.

In the United States in the late 1980's, one third of the major crops were lost to drought. At the same time in Germany, there was so much rain farmers had a hard time harvesting their crops. The winter of 1988 was the warmest one Japan had experienced up to that time. And 1988 also began a cycle of severe storms. Hurricane Gilbert of that year had the highest winds ever recorded in the Northern Hemisphere — 220 mph. But Gilbert was merely a warm-up for Hurricane Hugo in 1989. Hugo had "only" 175 mph winds, but caused unbelievable destruction because it hit so many land areas directly. It devastated the Caribbean and the Carolina coasts. Electricity was knocked out in many areas, and in some places, it took a month or more to repair. Water was contaminated. Some buildings were flattened and haven't been replaced because people did not have sufficient insurance to cover the damage. Hugo destroyed enough timber to build a city the size of Philadelphia.

This type of storm is going to increase in frequency and intensity as the changes continue. In part, this is because of the pollution we are putting into the air. We are warming the planet and changing the air currents. I warned people about this long before it happened. According to the Hopi prophecies, this is now the time when the seasons will change so much that we won't know one season from another.

Weather changes are going on all over the world. For example, in the late 1980's there was a four-inch snowfall in the Sahara Desert. This is something that has never happened before in recorded history. It is very interesting and very powerful that in the past few years we've been experiencing especially chilly weather in some unexpected places like Seattle, Washington. Yet, in other places like Spokane, where I come from, there has been a lot of unusually warm weather.

People in both these cities have also been concerned for a number of years that a major drought is already here. Do you wonder why? If you fly over the mountains of the western United States, you can see huge areas where all the trees have been cut down. Big timber companies logged them off without discrimination, without any sense of balance. That would have taken time and cost money. Now the tops of those mountains are desolate. Go and look, and you might find a little fringe of trees up against the road somewhere, but most of the land has been logged. So now that we don't have those great forests to hold the moisture in, droughts are coming with greater frequency.

Also in the late 1980's, southern California had great Santa Ana winds — the strongest and the worst ever. During this period I was driving to Palm Springs, and I pulled over beside a hill because the winds were so intense. I was going to rest in the van. Luckily, I looked up at the side of the hill and saw a vision of a major forest fire coming down it. I realized this was no place to rest, so I started heading down the freeway again.

While driving, I looked out across the city and saw a blinding flash as the winds knocked out an electrical transformer. Half of the city went black. This is another way the Earth changes work. I got down the road another 80 miles or so, and pulled off again. I listened to the radio and found out that the place where I had pulled over before had twenty houses burning as a result of a fire that had come down the side of the hill.

A few years back I had dreams — two in a row — about California. I dreamt that I was in southern California and there was snow on the ground. Shortly after my dreams, I went to southern California to do a workshop. The people who organized it for me were going to take me up to Big Bear Mountain for two days of meetings with the leaders of their group, but I said, "No way. I don't want to go up there. You're going to have a really heavy snow up there."

I said, "Let's go to Palm Springs." They agreed to Palm Springs because one of them had a condo there. We encountered four inches of snow on the way to Palm Springs. Big Bear had a blizzard. It was just like my dreams. In them, I also saw another thing that hasn't happened yet, but Spirit tells me it's going to come. I saw 150-foot waves hitting the California coast; they went way up the sides of the cliffs there.

Let's look at one connection between people and the weather. When it does snow, people often curse the snow. The snowplows come out as if they were removing some sort of bad disease. Many people have very negative feelings about snow. A lot of people feel negatively about rain as well. This isn't good. In the southeastern United States, there was a major drought because people weren't respectful of the forces. When they don't get respect, these powers withdraw. A few years back, New York City was on very heavy water rationing. Then Mayor Koch asked people to pray for rain. Someone did a good job, because they got rain. Their reservoirs became full again. Praying for rain and that kind of medicine can work no matter who does it, if they do it in a strong and proper manner.

Several years back it still hadn't snowed by the middle

of December at Lake Tahoe in Nevada — a great ski resort area. Resort owners contacted me. Somebody had told them there was an Indian who helped to bring the rain spirits, and they thought maybe he could do something to make it snow. So they invited me up to Lake Tahoe and gave me a big meal. Then they said, "Well, Sun Bear, we brought you up here because we need some help." I told them I would do a prayer and a ceremony and bring in some snow. In the next four days, I told them, they would have all the snow they needed — at least a foot and a half. And that's exactly what they got! The other powers that respond when I pray in a sacred manner are the winds and the thunder. On this continent and all over the world, the winds come up very strongly when I pray.

Shaking And Quaking

As the changes intensify, so will earthquakes, volcanic eruptions and other things having to do with Earth movement. In one 48-hour period in 1988, Japan was struck by 17,000 small earthquakes. These earthquakes broke up the water mains, caused gas leaks and disrupted all the transportation systems. These were just small ones. Wait until we get into the big earthquakes.

An earthquake that occurred off the coast of Madagascar raised the ocean floor 2,500 feet in one place and lowered it 1,500 feet in another. There is a tremendous amount of power in these forces as they begin shifting. I can foresee an earthquake in which all the land under city buildings would turn into liquid and act like water. This is called liquefaction, and it is a real threat. The buildings would sink in a matter of seconds.

In southern California millions of dollars are spent for earthquake detection. Small Richter scales and other earthquake detection devices are placed along major faults. This equipment tells scientists the strength of an earthquake — after it happens. That's a little late, as many San Franciscans discovered in 1989.

Do you know who can predict an earthquake before it happens? Our other relations. Cockroaches will spin around in circles announcing that an earthquake is coming. Catfish will stay completely dormant and the split-leaf philodendron will drop its leaves before a major earthquake. These are just some of the things in nature that send warning signals.

In China, a major earthquake in 1976 killed 800,000 people. Then another earthquake hit a few years later. The people were prepared for the second one and many lives were saved because they noticed the animals were starting to act restless, just as they had done before the 1976 earthquake.

What they've done in California as a result of this knowledge is to set up earthquake detection equipment at a zoo. They're beginning to think that maybe the animals know more about the coming of earthquakes than some of the professors at the colleges. Animals have an intuitive sense of these events. With it, they can alert people before the major changes happen — if the people will listen.

I remember first witnessing a volcanic eruption. It's a very powerful, very tremendous force. When some of my first apprentices started coming to learn from me, I told them, "I want you to keep your schedules open, because the time is going to come when I'm going to invite you to join me to watch a volcano erupt." I don't know if they really believed me or not.

But later I helped guide a tour in Hawaii during a period when the volcano Kilauea was active. I told the people on the tour that Kilauea was going to erupt again, and it did — for 22 hours. We got into a small plane and flew over the volcano. This great mountain with hot lava spewing 1,500 feet into the air was a powerful sight. It was beautiful to see the lava streaming down the side of the mountain at night. The air currents, which at one point made the plane drop 500 feet in a matter of seconds, were also exciting.

The Kahunas, the sacred teachers of Hawaii, have a lot of prophecies about volcanos. There are people in Hawaii, however, who don't believe these prophecies. The Kahunas warned one man not to build in a certain area because the land there belongs to Pele, the Volcano Goddess. He said, "Oh no, I've bought this land and I own it." He built a subdivision called the "Hawaiian Royal Gardens" on this land. But the Royal Gardens are much different now than when he built them — 75 of the houses are buried under volcanic lava. The Kahunas say Pele is eating the houses one at a time.

When another volcano erupted in 1973, it added 200 acres onto the Big Island! That shows the immense amount of lava that flowed into the ocean. The Hawaiian Islands belong to the volcanos — they don't belong to anybody else. The volcanos created the islands, and they rearrange them from time to time. The power of all volcanos is a very real thing and something we need to respect.

Spirit says all of this Earth movement is necessary for the survival of the planet. The reason it's necessary is that humans are not willing to make the necessary changes without being forced into them. They are too selfish and too greedy to give the Earth a rest where it is needed. People take and take from the Earth until they have completely destroyed all the natural force. If they are allowed to continue this behavior, then there is no possibility of a healthy balance being achieved. The Earth is making changes necessary for its survival, whether we humans are helping or not. My concern is to reach out to my brothers and sisters and make them aware of the Earth changes before they happen. By doing this, I'm helping them make the necessary changes in their lives.

Too Many People

The Bible says that in the beginning man and woman were created. Native American teachings say that the Great Spirit called the first man and the first woman into being a long, long time back. Whatever creation story you believe, it is obvious that man and woman got together and began to multiply.

By 1960 there were 3.7 billion people in the world. In 1989 we had 5 billion. The population of the world is now increasing at the rate of 70 million people a year. These are 70 million more people who are in need of all of the things that human beings require: food, shelter, air, water and whatever else it takes to live.

While Mr. Reagan was president, countries wanting to practice birth control because they weren't able to provide for their existing population were denied American help. This certainly helped the population explosion. So does the attitude of leaders who teach people to propagate for Father Church or the fatherland. And though many people would like to see a decrease in population growth — few are willing to limit the number of children they have themselves. We have effective methods of birth control but, unless we are willing to use them, we'll keep overpopulating until the Earth changes help us to come into balance.

Danger: Contaminated Areas

Let's take a look at worldwide pollution. There is a frightening amount of it. The chemical disasters that we've had already have been horrendous. The situation at Love Canal is a prime example of a very serious disaster. There they had to evacuate people from their homes when they discovered green ooze coming from swimming pools. The ooze originated from chemical dumps, where the waste seeped into the ground water.

Chemical pollution will be even worse in the future. A long time back, I had a powerful dream in which I saw signs posted in various parts of the world. The signs read, "Danger: Do Not Enter This Area Under Any Circumstances. It is Contaminated."

In 1984, I went to do a Medicine Wheel Gathering near St. Louis, Missouri. I saw the same sign which I had dreamed about along the freeway there. It warned people not to stop or get out of their cars under any circumstances, because that area was highly contaminated by the chemical dioxin. The area, called Times Beach, had been accidentally contaminated by a man who thought he was doing a public service by spraying the streets with pesticides to keep the mosquito population down.

In Thailand, there are no restrictions at all on pollution. Consequently, big chemical companies went in and abused the land to the point that they now have no pure water in any of the lakes or streams. All the water is polluted. The pollution has killed off many of the country's fish.

By 1990 the North Sea was dying. The whole sea was choking on too much algae, which cuts off oxygen. This algae is caused by pollution. In the late 1980's, a million and a half seals died off the coasts of Norway and Northern Europe because of various kinds of pollution.

In Germany, the Rhine River is so contaminated with chemical spills it is as good as dead. It is uninhabitable for any fish or wildlife for at least 25 years. And the water from the Rhine is moving out and polluting the water in other parts of Germany.

In coastal areas all over the world, the fishing fleets need to go out farther and farther because the natural resources close to shore have been decimated by pollution and over-fishing. We are destroying or using up everything in sight in the oceans as well as on the land.

In 1988 a major oil spill polluted the river systems through Pittsburgh, Pennsylvania. One and a half million gallons spilled there, wiping out a whole ecosystem.

Then the 1989 Exxon spill dumped 11.5 million gallons of oil off the coast of Alaska, killing thousands and thousands of creatures. The area will be polluted for many years to come. We need to document the far-reaching effects of such disasters so we can understand what went wrong and avoid repeating the same mistakes.

We have to be constantly aware of pollution so we can

stop it, and protect ourselves from the aftereffects of things that have already occurred. For instance, in many areas of the Earth you can't eat any of the fish from the rivers or the ocean. In other areas, you can't eat the fish once they get over five pounds because by then they are too contaminated. In some rivers, the fish have great sores on their bodies. This is part of the sickness we have put into the Earth and the water. And it's part of the sickness we're getting back.

Hardly A Drop To Drink

In the western United States many farms and farming areas are being abandoned because they don't have enough water anymore. The water table in the United States is dropping at the rate of a foot and a half each year in many areas and up to nine feet a year in others. By the late 1980's, arrangements were made so that you couldn't get water from the Colorado River and other sources if you didn't have water rights prior to the year 1910. As the end of the available water supply nears, government agencies are now saying that your water rights have to extend back for a certain period of time in order for you to have a right to the water.

The Bureau of Reclamation, which handles irrigation water systems, told farmers in California during the 1980's that they had to cut water usage by 50 percent. Since California raises a lot of the vegetable crops in the United States, cutting back on their water usage is cutting back on food.

It has been estimated that 93 percent of the water in the United States is contaminated. In Jacksonville, Florida, one river is so contaminated that fish have great holes and sores on their bodies. Yet at night, polluters still take their barges up the river with their lights off to dump even more chemicals into the river. In northern Florida, the ground water is so contaminated from the pesticides and chemicals used by agricultural and chemical industries that no one can drink

103

it. People have to be very careful when they buy land in that area because so much of the ground water is no longer usable. Similar things are happening all across the United States. In at least 33 major cities, the water is no longer fit to drink.

Because of the way we build huge irrigation systems in the Southwest — particularly in Arizona — water is now being pushed into dry, desert regions for irrigation. There, it is being sucked up by the sun through the evaporation process. Storm and rain clouds then develop and drop water out in other places. What is happening in India and elsewhere is that water which should be coming down on the land is falling in the ocean because of the imbalances that humans have created in nature. All of these imbalances are becoming more prevalent.

The situation with the air isn't any better. There hasn't been any pure air for a while now. The last pure air was found in the mountains of New Mexico back in 1961.

As I travelled across the continental United States, I used to say the only place where there was smog was Los Angeles. Now most major cities have smog problems. Spokane, Washington, has a smog alert every other day. Reno, Nevada, has a serious smog problem too. It's hard to find any place where the air is clear and smog-less — whether you are in the United States, Europe, or the urban areas of Latin America.

Gold Or Wheat?

In both 1987 and 1988, people consumed more food than they produced. In mid-1989, it was estimated that the world had only a 58-day supply of grain left. The Russians and Chinese, with even smaller supplies, were buying all they could. China was suffering from a major drought and famine was a real possibility there. Much of Eastern Europe and Russia were rationing food. The rationing was increasing to include more foods every day.

1988 was the second year in a row that the world

consumed more food than it produced. It was also the year of the most extensive drought in history. The United States lost a third of its crops to drought that year. And the Quaker Oats Company, for the first time, had to go outside of the United States to buy oats.

In 1989 the United States had 500 million bushels of grain in reserve but needed 750 million to feed the country. Because of the aftereffects of the Chernobyl nuclear disaster, the Russians were still buying wheat from the United States. The Russians sold a lot of gold because they wanted to eat.

Similar situations are happening in many other places. In Latin America, many terrorist organizations kill farmers and people who are trying to organize farm cooperatives, because they want to keep their country in chaos. Starving people are open to any philosophy that will give them food.

In the United States, much of the wheat and grain crops were threatened in the late 1980's by what is called the Siberian wheat mite. This insect is so clever that agribusiness can't get it even with all of their pesticides. It burrows into the ground during the daytime when they're spraying and only comes up at night to feed, so the sprays just don't meet up with him.

Back in 1970, farmers in the South lost 75 percent of their corn crop because of a disease called smut. They simply weren't able to control it. It just blew from one field to another and spread all across the South. Later, a similar problem occurred in Idaho. There they had both potato rot and onion rot. They had to abandon whole fields. Crops can't be grown in these fields anymore because the soil has been so contaminated with these sicknesses.

In the United States and Europe, hybrid plants have been developed to produce high crop yields. But they have bred the immunities out of these plants in the process. Many of them can no longer fight off insects, molds or other pests. Also, the seeds have been developed to work best with chemical fertilizers and pesticides.

Another thing to keep in mind about hybrid plants is that you can harvest the plants, but their seed is no good to plant. You have to go back to the seed companies to plant next year's crop. So the seeds, in reality, are owned by these companies, which are owned by the multinational corporations. Since these companies have a monopoly on hybrid seeds, farmers are finding that prices are going up every year. Garden seeds which used to cost five cents a package now cost $1.35. Yet the farmers are getting the same for what they sell. It's as if there is a guy standing with a gun at the farmer's head saying, "You can't farm unless you buy my seed."

Can you see what this means? We humans are continuing to become more and more dependent on things beyond our control. To counterbalance this trend, many of us have set up non-hybrid seed banks where we distribute seeds for free. People who use the seeds donate some back after their harvest so we can keep the seed bank going. In this way we can help our brothers and sisters stay alive on the planet.

It is very frightening that we are dependent on gasoline-driven engines and petroleum-based chemicals for our farming. I look around and wonder what will happen in the United States, Europe and elsewhere when there is no petroleum. At one time, I could go into certain areas and see a few people still using draft horses to raise their crops. That's not true anymore. This is a very dangerous time because we are totally dependent on the oil companies for our food supply — and they are largely dependent on oil from the Middle East. We need to look carefully at these things and be aware of what is happening.

Creating Imbalance
In the fall of 1973 in northern California, 100 million mice invaded Tule Lake. The folks who lived there were asking for people to send cats. They were using every means possible to kill the mice — clubbing them, digging ditches,

anything they could think of to get rid of them.

In 1984 in southern Idaho, more than a million jack rabbits were creating havoc with the crops. The farmers said the rabbits were doing $5 million in damage a year. Farmers were lining up rabbit drives to club the rabbits to death by the thousands. They killed 85,000 rabbits one weekend, and 90,000 another weekend. The killing went on like this, with clubbing and poison-laced alfalfa pellets, until the farmers had killed one million rabbits.

Why were there all those surplus rabbits? Why 100 million mice? The answer is because the same ranchers and farmers had killed every hawk, owl, skunk and coyote — all the wild, natural predators that keep the balance in nature. That's why. We create imbalances in nature, and then we have to suffer the consequences. What will thrive next in the absence of all the mice and rabbits?

Because of humans, the cycles of many animals, in addition to mice and rabbits, are out of balance. I've seen many animals bear their young, then refuse to look after them and nurse them. This is happening with both farm and wild animals. Because the elements are so pushed out of balance, the animals are losing their ability to work in harmony.

So are the plants. We are seeing the trees bud in northern areas during unseasonably warm weather in the winter, sometimes as early as February. Then a heavy frost comes along and freezes them up again. This can mean the end of the fruit crop for that year.

The imbalance also extends to humans. Major illnesses heretofore unknown are one of the biggest dangers that I foresee. Some will be caused by the pollutants humans have put into the land. Combinations of pollutants bring new diseases. AIDS is just a forerunner of what will come. There will soon be other diseases over which we have no control.

The chemicals we have used in our food chain have weakened it. Much of the food we get now doesn't have any natural nutrients. We've worn out the soil and haven't put the proper nutrients back into it. Most of the food is harvested before it has had time to ripen, so it lacks the natural power it would otherwise have. I see the stamina of many humans weakening because of this food.

It is also true, in many parts of the world today, that people have gotten sucked into the fast foods, the processed foods, and they don't have the stamina that they once had. A while back, I had two young men come out and cut wood with me. They were with me to learn spiritual things. I said, "Here's the first spiritual thing that we are going to do. We are going to cut the wood here in this woodpile." In a short time they were both worn-out. They said, "Sun Bear, this is hard work. Can't we take a break?" And I said, "Oh, I know who you are. You're the fast food generation. You don't have power or stamina because you don't eat the right kinds of food." Improper nutritional habits will definitely contribute to the pestilence I see coming.

I also see major problems with the immune systems of people because they have been overly sanitized for so long. They don't have much resistance to natural germs. When I was a young child, I used to go barefoot. I'd walk in the cow and horse manure in the barnyards, and cut my feet with sticks, stones and glass. As a result, my body has built up its natural immune system. I have a lot of resistance to things that other people do not have.

All the things that I have told you about in this chapter are happening because of the imbalances created by what humans have done to the Earth and to themselves. This death culture activity has set up an imbalance in nature, and among humankind. And the vicious cycle continues, making the coming changes even more necessary.

Chapter Six

When The Dinosaurs Fall

In order to see fully what is happening on the Earth, we have to take a look at those human beings who are causing the destruction of their fellow human beings. In olden times, the same sort of people engineered the destruction of the Native peoples, almost bringing them to total extinction. That shows how their minds worked then.

These mental patterns go way, way back in human history. They go back to a time when some tribes decided that they each had the absolute right to destroy anybody else who didn't share their particular spiritual belief or race. These tribespeople felt that they had some god-given right to destroy. We need to look at this now because many people today still have this way of thinking.

For historical examples of what I mean, we can go back to the ancient Hebrews. They felt *they* were the chosen people. But then so did the other tribes around them, including the Philistines. All these people regarded the same land as their territory and believed any interlopers should be destroyed.

Another example is the ancient King of Assyria, who regarded himself as "Lord of the Earth." As such, he felt he had the right to conquer all the nations around him. He had no regard for other people as long as his own path prospered. The Egyptian Pharaohs were other "rulers of divine right" who carried on their bloodbaths of conquest and then, ultimately, enslaved the people around them to build their pyramids and other monuments.

Later in history we had the "glorious" Roman Empire. It provides another story of enslavement. The Romans sought control over other peoples' lives. They felt they had the supreme right to do whatever they wanted because they ruled by some "divine right of the gods." Anybody who opposed them, or didn't find harmony with their purpose, was thrown to the lions or destroyed in some other way.

Then, we had the so-called "Christian Church." Once the church leaders believed they had their full power (particularly the Catholic Church), they killed anybody who didn't agree with them. Those who didn't follow their particular beliefs were subject to the "Holy Inquisition" — through which the church tortured, murdered and destroyed millions of people in the name of God. Some historians say nine million people were murdered in Europe during the Inquisition. They were killed because they didn't follow the particular spiritual belief system of the dominant culture. I always wonder what Jesus thinks of those people claiming to follow his example by marching forward with a cross on their banners reading, "By this sign we conquer."

At the same time the Christians were marching, so were the Moslems. Mohammed, the head of the holy Moslem religion, preached conquest by the sword and by submission. The Moslem teachings were spread over many areas by the sword. Tens of thousands of people were killed because they didn't believe what the Moslems told them to.

Then we can look at China, where the great conquerors waged war on any people who opposed their beliefs. Genghis Khan and Tamerlane were two good examples of this.

There were many other people in the world who believed they had the right to tell everyone else how to live. For example, look at Central and South America. First there were the Incas, who felt they were the lords of the world. That gave them the "right" to enslave or kill any people who opposed them. The Aztecs said they were the gods, the "Sons of the Sun." They believed that other tribal people were there to be slaves or sacrifices for their temples.

This is but a small part of the bloody history of humanity. For most of recorded time, everybody has wanted to be top dog and has tried to destroy anybody else who didn't agree with their particular teachings or beliefs. We need to look at this behavior very carefully, because this is the bloody way humans have used their power. They have used it to destroy.

Now, let's go further back in time and look at the period when the Native Americans lived alone in North America. Many tribes were scattered over large areas. There was only limited warfare. Each tribe had an area that was given to them by the Great Spirit, and most of them didn't really think they were so superior to anybody else. Admittedly, some did. This little germ of arrogance — so common in the world — prevailed in some places in North America also.

Then into this relatively tranquil setting came the "Great European Conquerors." First came the conquistadores, the Spaniards. They said, "For God, Glory and Country." Then they slaughtered as many Indians as possible for gold, God, glory and their homeland. They murdered millions of Native people in Mexico and South America. They enslaved others and used them in any way that they wanted, feeling righteous as they did it because they believed the Christian God was blessing them.

As one historian put it, "First the Europeans fell on their knees — then they fell on the Indians." All these European people were of various so-called religious persuasions. Many of them said that they were leaving Europe to escape religious persecution. Yet these same people were totally intolerant of Native American people and their spirituality, or even of their right to live upon the land. The Europeans felt when they came here that they had a "manifest destiny" which gave them the right to conquer this whole land "from sea to shining sea." They thought it also gave them the right to murder off all of the Indians in the way of "destiny." As I said earlier, the Indian population in the United States area was reduced from 3 million in the 1600's to 300,000 by 1900. The basic philosophy of the United States government — and the French and English before them — was expressed by a general who said, "The only good Indian is a dead Indian." Or as another general said when authorizing his troops to slaughter women and children, including little babies, along with any warriors,

"Nits make lice. Kill them all."

This is another part of the bloody history of humanity. It is depressing, tracing it down, to look at what has happened over and over again. In the name of "God" and "Country," humans have consistently tried to destroy their fellow human beings upon this planet. Ernest Seton, the man who founded the Woodcraft Rangers, turned away from the Boy Scouts after he had started them up in the United States. He stated that more people had been murdered in the name of God and country than for any other purpose. Consequently, he didn't want to be part of the organization when it incorporated patriotism as a way of inspiring young people. He felt that true spirituality began with patriotism to the Earth Mother and to our fellow human beings upon the Earth.

Progress?

The mass murders perpetrated by so-called modern civilization are another example of what I'm talking about. Adolf Hitler killed six and a half million Jews, and many millions of Polish, Russian, Slavic and other people, because he felt they were sub-human beings. He thought his was the superior race and believed that this supposed superiority gave him the right to murder all of those other peoples. Hitler was prepared to destroy whole populations all over Europe so he would have space to build up his super-race. And he came to power without much resistance from the German people or their allies.

When the Hitler regime started, the other so-called civilized nations did very little to stop it. They saw what was happening, and allowed it to continue. At the time when Hitler's rule was still weak and he was just starting to take over other lands and kill off people, nothing was said or done by England or the United States. They didn't respond until it got to the point of threatening their own worlds. We need to look at this to see how "good, concerned" people allow dictators to come in and take power.

Let's not forget Mr. Stalin in Russia. In early 1990, Soviet authorities finally admitted that under Mr. Stalin's rule as many as 60 million people perished. He murdered millions of his own people directly and caused untold other deaths by starvation or "relocation" programs. He wiped out whole populations who didn't agree with him and his policies.

Mr. Khomeini is another person who murdered off thousands of people who didn't agree with him. While he was alive, he'd kill anyone he could who had a different spiritual belief. And as I write this book, there are people in Ireland, Africa, Latin America, the Middle East, the Orient, and America who are murdering each other over religious and/or patriotic beliefs. And people wonder why the Earth changes are necessary!

Let us look at Africa. Thousands of Africans were killed at the dictate of Mr. Idi Amin. Ethiopia is murdering off its own people because of political and spiritual differences. In South Africa, the small white minority is murdering people just because they are black. In the United States, people are still being murdered because of their race or kept in a state of poverty that causes slow death. In Brazil, Mexico, Peru, El Salvador, Nicaragua — in all of Central and South America — Native Indian people are still being murdered and their land taken from them.

We need to look at these things very carefully. These are events that have happened — and are still happening — in our time, in this era of "advanced civilization." We need to acknowledge all these things so that we can attempt to understand all the destructive ways in which human beings behave toward each other. We need to look at the mental attitudes that continually perpetuate human misery. Through such an understanding, we might begin to change the underlying attitudes.

Let's look at what is happening in Israel. The Israelis are now murdering off thousands of Palestinian people and forcing them to be landless. Why? Because the Palestinians think and believe differently than the Israelis do. But both of these peoples are equally guilty of perpetrating the sorts of crimes that humans have committed against other humans throughout history. As long as this kind of a spirit is loose upon the Earth, we must make every effort to stop it.

We also need to look at Lebanon. Because of religious and political differences, groups there are murdering each other off. This murder happens because one is a Moslem of one sect and another is of a different sect. I asked the Creator, "What is this that is happening in Lebanon?" The Creator said, "It is very simple. You give two violent people guns and they kill each other. The killing continues as long as there are violent people." The Arabs say when a boy is born, "Another gun for Allah." This is the mentality that prevails in many parts of the world where it's okay to kill somebody who is not of your spiritual belief or race. This is the sickness that is upon the Earth. We need to keep this in mind to understand what the cleansing of the Earth is really about.

And don't be naive enough to believe there are any countries that have not committed atrocities during war. During World War II, the Allies committed atrocities against soldiers and civilians alike. They rounded the Japanese up and tortured and mistreated them in their prison camps. American soldiers would sometimes slit the throats of Japanese captives to see how far they could run before they bled to death. I was told this by a marine who said this was one of their favorite sports. During the Vietnam War, we weren't able to overlook the atrocities committed by American soldiers. The so-called good Christian boys from America would slaughter all the people in a village after they had had the pretty women. They would murder them just because they happened to be Vietnamese. We need to remember these things. They are part of the indictment that tells what we humans are responsible for upon the Earth.

Then look at the thinking that has allowed this. Look

115

at the conditioning that has been put upon us by our leaders. Our religious leaders tell us anybody who doesn't belong to our religion is fair game to be our victim. The politicians who refer to other people as "foreigners" feel they have a right to do anything they want with these people. This attitude is indicative of racism and nationalism, which are the deepest sicknesses of humanity. They are causing much of the destruction on the planet today; they have caused the enslavement and the debasement of all races of humans. Part of the cleansing is about freeing people from all this racism and nationalism and from the arrogance of some humans who put themselves above others.

In their senseless wars, humans are also destroying the Earth. In modern warfare, the problem isn't only what happens to the humans — it's what happens to the other kingdoms also. Think of the water pollution that the uncaring people of Iran and Iraq caused by sinking ships that were carrying oil. Think of all the innocent wild creatures of the ocean which were destroyed during just one senseless battle. Multiply it by all the other similar incidents and you'll see that the foolish things humans are doing to each other are also destroying the planet.

Who Are The Poor People?

As the Earth changes intensify, a lot of people in this country are going to find out quickly that they're the poor people. I was down in South America with a group of 35 North Americans a while back. They were looking at the Mayan Indians in the jungle down there, and some were calling them "poor." But the Mayans can put up a house in about three or four days. They put some poles into the ground, put up some cross poles, and then some slanted poles on top to make a roof. They add a couple of poles for a doorway if they want to get a little fancier. Then they thatch the whole thing with grass, and in three or four days have a house built. If they want to keep the chickens and turkeys out, they put a few more poles around the sides. It's not very fancy but it didn't cost $100,000!

I told the folks with me that these Mayans aren't the poor people. They were going to raise a corn crop that year just like they did last year and the year before. They don't care about what's happening in Guatemala City, because they don't need anything from the government. The Guatemalan government doesn't tax their corn crop, because they don't want to go into the jungle to collect taxes. So the Mayans are living just as they always have.

The poor people, the people I really feel sorry for, are the folks in the United States who have solidly pinned themselves into believing that the dominant system is real. I see the Mayan people coming into the city with their extra corn to sell, in bags on their backs. They made the bags themselves. These people don't have a problem with their way of life. No matter what happens in other parts of the world, they are going to eat. Their lives will continue.

Being independent like the Mayans is part of what I'm trying to teach people right now, because I live totally against the grain of this whole society. Everybody says, "Oh, get more credit. Get more credit." Yet the poor babies in this country are credited up to their eyebrows! Back in the late 1930's and early 1940's, my sister would go to school with patches on her Levi's and some of the kids would make fun of her. "Well," she said, "at least the bill collectors from Spiegel's aren't after these jeans!"

My relationship with the United States government is very limited. I abide by the country's laws, but I don't put any other energy into it. I just hope that when the government falls, along with the other dinosaurs, it doesn't fall on top of me! That's the only thing I'm concerned about. I don't petition the United States government for anything because, to me, it's like kicking a dying horse and asking it to dance a little bit more.

If I were going to be political in the 1990's, however, I would find people interested in creating a politically conscious group that represented a very specific concept and purpose. I would find people, whether they were Republicans or Democrats, who would go out and say, "Hey, this is what we want." I would create a united front to get our message to the politicians in a strong enough manner for us to be heard. If nothing else, such groups — perhaps organized around specific environmental issues — would confront some issues with strong energy, get rid of some frustrations, and wake the politicians up a little bit.

But I'm not interested in being political. Instead, my energy is focused on helping to create a different way of life, a way that's new, alive and real. That's what we've been doing at the Bear Tribe for the last 20 years. At this point, we've gotten past the adolescent stage and now the community is a place where people involved with it are successful and happy. Everybody's eating regularly, and it works well for those living there and those connected with the Tribe in other ways. One of our efforts, *Wildfire* magazine, is published to show people how we can come together and look at ways to effectively solve problems. In the programs we offer at Vision Mountain and around the world, we work directly with people to help them develop in practical and spiritual ways so they can really help themselves, and others. So we're not crawling into our dens and crying; we're actively creating changes.

Political Chaos

I see a lot of political unrest and chaos coming, as well as major economic problems. You are looking at some very powerful changes; be aware of that. Many countries are facing chaos on account of political problems. At the beginning of 1990 there was continuing unrest in Russia. Moslems were in conflict in Lebanon. Tension between Iran and Iraq continued, and Iraq was causing much unease throughout the world. Latin America was in turmoil.

One thing that happens when there is political chaos is that people don't get around to raising much food. They are so worried about whether someone is going to shoot them, or that something else might happen, that they don't put their time into raising food. That means famine. This is the situation in Africa. One of the major disruptive factors, besides the drought, is that so many factions are busy fighting each other people never have a chance to feel safe enough to plant a crop. In Ethiopia and the Sudan many people don't even bother to plant a crop because they don't know if they'll be able to harvest it. Farming is of little value to them.

Both Russia and the United States are getting out of the role of helping Third World countries. The two "super powers" don't have the resources anymore, and neither does anyone else. Withdrawal of aid by the West started in the Sudan, Chad, and Ethiopia. By 1990, Russia and the United States were pulling back on military and economic aid to many countries. This is why they are asking these countries to resolve their own conflicts.

Something I've been saying for a long time is beginning to appear more possible now. I have not foreseen a nuclear confrontation between the U.S. and Russia, probably because they have been so evenly matched. But I've seen the possibility of smaller nuclear wars, such as between the Arabs and Israel. Now we find that Israel has maybe a hundred atomic bombs. Iraq is trying hard to get their own bombs. I think that if tensions over there increase too much, either of these countries would use them. That, of course, will affect everyone.

Gold Or Faith?

There's a lot wrong, too, with the worldwide economy. Most currencies are backed only by faith and prayer. The developed nations have loaned money to the developing ones with no chance of getting it back. They've already had to write off billions.

I asked a good brother of mine, who works with one of the top banks in the world, what the economy was really like. He said, "It is very, very nervous; one little cough and it's down!" That was his feeling about it. Part of what is happening at this time is that the banks have had their sugar plums disappear. They don't have anything they can really make money on like they used to. Then we have all of our dear brothers and sisters who have borrowed up to their ears with equity loans on their houses. When the interest rates start going up, it's going to be very difficult for them. The inevitable collapse of the savings and loan industry will cost the American taxpayers $500 billion or more. And then the next bunch to watch will be those corporations which were taken over by junk bond sales.

I'm often reminded of the story about the old Indian chief who said, "Well, my people, I've got some good news and some bad news." He said, "This year has been a tough year and we won't have anything to eat this winter except buffalo chips!" They asked, "What's the good news?" He said, "There's plenty of buffalo chips!" That's the kind of economic future we could easily see before the year 2000.

Attitudes To Help

Economically, we need to start learning some very important lessons. One of them is how to shift dependencies from a system that is becoming less dependable all the time to depending upon each other and the Earth Mother. To me that means finding people you can work with and forming communities. I don't mean that you all have to live in the same house, but you must learn to have alliances with people.

As an example, the way the Bear Tribe operates is that some people work at our office in the city, bringing in the cash flow to the Tribe; other people work at the farm, growing food and developing the land base so we can be more self-sufficient. This linkage between the two groups keeps everybody employed, eating good food — at times we've produced 80 percent of our own food — and moving cooperatively in the same direction. As the Earth changes intensify, we're developing the ability to do more of our work on the mountain so we're not caught in a dependence on the city.

We're also in the process of helping to create a network of communities across the country and in other parts of the world. The reason that we're doing this is because Spirit told me to go out and help people raise their level of consciousness. After they get a little brighter, the next step is to keep them alive during the time of the changes. I'm trying to teach people a lot of things in a very short period of time, because we only have a short time.

Technology: Friend Or Foe?

To me, technology is something that is fine to use, wisely. The misuse of it is something else. We have to be aware of what we do with technology and how much it's costing us. I'm not speaking of dollars and cents; I'm speaking of how much it costs us in terms of the environment, our health, and in other ways. Beware of that. It is very important that we know how much we are "paying" for the technology we use.

I was doing a lecture at an ashram in Los Angeles once, and the people there thought I wasn't politically aware enough. They asked me if I had a petition for them to sign to stop the mining of coal at Black Mesa by the Peabody Coal Company. They were giving me a lot of dialogue as to why I should be getting a petition out. I asked them, "Do you really want to stop the mining in Black Mesa?" They said, "Oh yes, yes we do." I said, "Okay, here's all you have to do." And I reached over and turned off the light switch! I told them this is a world of supply and demand. If you are demanding more power and you're willing to pay for it, they are going to mine Black Mesa to bring that power to you. When you are ready to take more responsibility for your life and say, "No, I'll do without that electricity," then that mining is not going to happen anymore.

I have nothing against the lightbulb. I fly in jet airplanes. I use an automobile. I'm honest about what I use. Sometimes people like to play that they're holy. I ask them, "How did you get here today, brother, sister? Tell me about it. Where's your horse?"

Look at technology and utilize it in a sacred manner. You can have a car, but use it in such a way that you get the most value out of it; share a ride with somebody. Turn off lights that you're not using. Don't flush the toilet every time you use it. In little ways like that, you are taking responsibility for your life and using technology in a responsible manner.

Just don't become too dependent on technology. Be careful not to get to the point where everything works only with the computer. Then if the computer doesn't work, you're in bad shape. Don't be dependent on systems that are beyond your control; that's where the real danger lies. If you turn the faucet on and the water doesn't come out of the pipes, you're in bad shape. If something happens to the electricity, the gas, the oil, and you don't know how else to cook or keep warm, you'll have a real problem. When the gasoline pumps don't work down at the service stations, you're going to be hurting.

I look at the big cities in the world and, to me, they are death traps. Once everything comes down and chaos begins, I don't see anybody in the cities getting more than 25 miles outside of the city limits. The problem with cities stems from all the things that they're dependent on technology for. When the Earth changes intensify, the urban areas, which worship technology, just might find that their god has turned against them.

Chapter Seven

How Dinosaurs Die

Many of you may believe that the Earth changes are coming but wonder just how systems in a civilized country could fall apart. In this chapter I'm going to give you scenarios from two people I respect. One is Bill Mollison, the developer of a sustainable approach to agriculture which he calls permaculture. His views which follow are excerpted from his pamphlet entitled, "An Introduction to Permaculture."*

The real systems that are beginning to fail [on the Earth] are the soils, forests, the atmosphere, and the nutrient cycle systems. And it is we who are responsible for that. We haven't evolved anywhere in the West (and I doubt very much elsewhere except in tribal areas) any sustainable systems in agriculture or forestry. We don't have a system. Let's look at what's happening.

Forests have been found to be far more important in the oxygen cycle than we ever suspected. We used to think oceans were the most important element. They are not. Not only are they not very important, contributing probably less than eight percent of the oxygen in the atmospheric recycling, but many are beginning to be oxygen consuming. If we release more mercury into the seas, the oceans will be oxygen consuming. The balance is changing. Therefore, it is mainly the forests that we depend on to preserve us from an anarchic condition.

Of the forests, some are critically important, like the evergreen forests, of which there are two extensive systems. One is equatorial, multi-species; and the other, the cool evergreen forests of the Russian tundra and the southern evergreen forests. Rain forests are critically important in the oxygen cycle, and in atmospheric stability.

* Available from Yankee Permaculture, Box 202, Orange, MA 01364. Write them for price and more information.

The forests also provide a very large amount of our precipitation. When you cut the forest from ridges, you can observe the rainfall itself decrease between 10 percent and 30 percent, which you could possibly tolerate. What you don't see happen is that the precipitation may decrease over 86 percent, the rainfall being only a small fraction of the total precipitation. It is quite possible on quiet clear nights with no cloud, no rainfall recorded anywhere on any gauges, to have a major precipitation in forest systems. It is particularly true of maritime climates. But it is also true of all climates. Therefore, it is possible to very rapidly produce semi-desert conditions simply by clearing trees from ridge tops. This is being done at a great rate.

It is the character of the forest to moderate everything. Forests moderate excessive cold and heat, excessive run-off, excessive pollution; and as they are removed, immoderate extremes arrive. And of course, it is the forests that create soils. They are one of the very few soil-creating systems that there are.

What is happening to the forests? We use a great many forest products in a very temporary way — paper, and particularly newspaper. The demand has become excessive. At present we are cutting one million hectares per annum in excess of planting. But in any one month that can rapidly change.

Of all the forests that we ever had, as little as two percent remain in Europe. I don't think there is a tree in Europe that doesn't exist because of the tolerance of man or that hasn't been planted by man. There is no such thing as a primeval European forest. As little as eight percent remain in South America. And 15 percent, I think, is a general figure in other areas. So we have already destroyed the majority of forests, and we are working on a rather minor remnant. Cutting rates vary, depending on the management practices. But in general, even in South America, and throughout the Third World, and wherever multinationals can obtain ownership of forest in the Western World, it is about a 100 percent loss. It is a "cut and run" system.

We have long been lulled into a very false sense of security by reassurances that the logging companies are planting eight trees for a tree cut. What we are really interested in is biomass. When you take something out of the forest in excess of 150 tons, and put something back which doesn't weigh more than ten ounces, you are not in any way preserving biomass.

What are the uses to which we put forests? The major uses are as newsprint and packaging material. Even the few remaining primeval forests are being cut for this. Forests that had never seen the footsteps of man, that had never experienced any human interference, are being cut for newsprint. Those are forests in which the trees may be two hundred feet to the first branch, gigantic cathedrals. They are being cut and shipped out as chips. So, for the most part, we are degrading the primeval forests to the lowest possible use.

That has effects at the other end of the system. Waste products from forests are killing large areas of the sea. The main reason why the Baltic and the Mediterranean and the coast off New York have become oxygen consuming is that we are carpeting the sea bottom with forest products. There are, broadly speaking, about twelve thousand billion tons of carbon dioxide being released annually by the death of forests. We are dependent on the forests to lock up the carbon dioxide. In destroying forests, we are destroying the system which should be helping us. We are working on a remnant of the system. It is this last remnant which is being eroded.

The effects of this on world climate are becoming apparent both in the composition of the atmosphere and in the inability of the atmosphere to buffer changes. In any month now we will break the world records in some weather way or another. In my [Australian] home town we are very isolated and buffered by ocean and forest, but we had in succession the windiest, the driest, and the wettest month in history, in two hundred years of recording. So really what's happening in the world climate is not that it is tending towards the greenhouse effect; it is not that it is tending toward the ice age; it is starting now to fluctuate so wildly that it is totally unpredictable as to which heat barrier you will crack; but when you crack it, you will crack it in extreme, and you will crack it very suddenly, and it will be a very sudden change that takes place. Until then, we will experience immense variability in climate.

We can just go cutting along, and in maybe twelve more years we won't have any forests.

There is still another factor. It would be bad enough if it was just our cutting that is killing off forests. But since the 1920's, and with increasing frequency, we have been losing species from forests to a whole succession of pathogens. It started with things like chestnut blight. Chestnuts were 80 percent of the forests that they occupied. So a single species dropping out may represent enormous biomass, enormous biological reserve, and a very important tree. Now, curiously enough (and not noticed by most people, but now pointed out by Richard St. Barbe Baker), is that the trees that are going are those with the greatest leaf area per unit. First, chestnuts, with maybe sixty acres of leaf area per tree. Then the elms, running about forty. Now even the beeches are going, and the oaks, the eucalyptus in Australia and Tasmania. Even the needle leaf trees in Japan are failing. The Japanese coniferous forests are going at a fantastic rate; so are the Canadian shield forests and the Russian forests.

Now, we come to a thing we are calling *the phas-*

mid conspiracy. Each forest varies in each country in that its elms, its chestnuts, its poplars, and its firs are subject to attack by specific pathogens. Insects are taking some sort of cauterizing measures. The American reaction would be to spray; the British reaction would be to fell and burn; and in Australia, the reaction is to say, "Ah, what the Hell! It's going to be gone next year, let it go!"

Really, is it these diseases? What are the diseases? Phasmids are responsible for the death of eucalyptus. There is the cinnamon fungus. In elms, it's the Dutch elm disease. In the poplars, it's the rust. And in the firs, it's also rust. Do you think any of these diseases are killing the forest? What I think we are looking at is a carcass. The forest is a dying system on which the decomposers are beginning to feed. If you know forests very well, you know that you can go out this morning and strike a tree with an axe. That's it. Or touch it with the edge of a bulldozer, or bump it with your car; and then if you sit patiently by that tree, within three days you will see that maybe twenty insects and other decomposers and "pests" have visited the injury, and the tree is already doomed. What attracts them is the smell from the dying tree. We have that in Australia, because we have noticed it. Just injure trees to see what happens, and the phasmids come. The phasmid detects the smell of this. The tree has become its food tree, and it comes to feed. So whatever the gypsy moth is doing, it is coming in at the right time to clean up the tree and decompose it rapidly so that new life-cycles can begin. But we spray gypsy moth, and this affects an enormous number of checks and balances.

So insects are not the *cause* of the death of forests. The cause of the death of forests is multiple insult. We point to some bug, and we say, "That bug did it." It is much better if you can blame somebody else. You all know that. So we blame the bug. It is a conspiracy, really, to blame the bugs. But the real reason the trees are failing is that there have been profound changes in the amount of light penetrating the forest, in pollutants, and in acid rain fallout. People, not bugs, are killing the forests.

The Soil

We have lost 50 percent of all the soils we have ever had before 1950. We have been measuring pretty well since 1950. And we have lost 30 percent of the soils we had in 1950, and we will inevitably lose another 30 percent of the soils that remain. Now this is as true of the Third World as it is in the Western World.

The rate at which soils are created is at about four tons per annum per acre — much less in dry areas. These soils are created by the fall of rain and the action of the plants. That rate varies. In the desert, they are being created at a much lesser rate; but in these humid climates, at about four tons per acre. If you don't lose any more than four tons of soil per acre per annum, you are on a break-even. But let us have a look at the usual thing; in Australia we lose about twenty-seven tons of soil per cultivated acre per annum. America, however, where they grow corn, can lose as much as four hundred tons per acre per annum. While the average may be twenty, it will go as high as four hundred or five hundred tons. In Canada, they are measuring the humus loss, and that is about the same. There, they are running out of humus. In the prairies, where they started with good humic soils, they are now down to a mineral soil base.

Here is something that should be of interest to each of us. For every head of population — whether you are an American or an East Indian — if you are a grain eater, it now costs about twelve tons of soil per person per year for us to eat grain. All this loss is a result of tillage in agriculture. As long as you are tilling, you are losing. At the rate we are losing soils, we don't see that we will have agricultural soils within a decade.

Apart from the soils we are losing directly by tillage, we are losing enormous quantities of soils to what is called desertification. In the state of Victoria, in Australia, we are losing eight hundred thousand acres [in some] years to salt. That means not only a loss of soils which are tilled, but also a loss of the soils that we don't till, soils that are tending to disappear from agriculture on their own accord.

Now the main reason for soils disappearing is the cutting of forest. And almost always the cutting of forest is remote from the site where the soil is lost. That is, you can do nothing if your soil starts to turn salty here, because the reason lies way up the watershed, maybe a thousand miles away. We are starting to get soil salting in humid climates in Australia. It is becoming a "factor out of place." It is not only occurring in deserts. It is occurring in quite humid, winter-wet climates. How did that happen?

It is not a simple process, but it is easily understood. The rainfall, as it falls on hills and penetrates forests, has a net downward transfer. If we remove forests, what we now have is a net evaporation loss. Forests transmit clean water down, and they release clean water into the atmosphere. This net downward transfer carries with it the salts which are an inevitable part of that additional four tons of soil per acre which is produced from broken down rocks. These salts normally travel on out in what we could characterize as deep leads. They are not surface systems. Fresh water runs off the surface and soaks down. Even in humid climates, we have much saltier water at depth than we have on the surface. This is because the trees act as pumps to keep the deep leads low. That's the whole process.

If we cut the trees down, the deep leads rise at a measurable rate, and they are rising measurably across enormous areas in America, Africa and Australia. When they are up to about three feet below the surface, the trees start to die of "phasmids"; and when they are up to about eighteen inches below the surface, other crops start to die; and when they reach the surface, they evaporate, and the soil visibly goes to salt. Then the Australian government starts providing free pumps to farmers, and they start pumping out the salt water. Where can they discard the water they pump out? Big problem.

The next step is to have concrete delivered in, so it will now be water diverted from the rivers that soaks into the soil, while they are pumping the salt water off into the sea. And they have to be doing that forever. You now want a thousand pumps. At the same time that the government is supplying pumps to farmers, they are leasing additional wood-chopping licenses to the multinationals, who are doing very well. They are selling pumps on one hand and wood chips on the other. It is a happy circumstance for some people, but a catastrophe for the Earth.

We are losing soils and increasing desert at a simply terrifying rate. And that is without any plowing for agriculture. You ask if the analysts of the multinational firms are aware of these problems? No, they have degrees in economics and business management and all sorts of irrelevant areas.

Mining is also a major factor in salting on a local basis, and has accounted on its own for the whole loss of hardwood forests in areas of western Australia, and no doubt elsewhere. Mining brings up a lot of residues which are evaporated on the surface.

The largest single factor in Britain causing loss of

soils is the construction of highways. It is also a major factor in America. In Britain, I think there is a mile of highway for every square mile of surface. And highways are being rapidly extended on the supposition that you will never need the soil, and that highways will enable you to increase energy use. Highways account for permanent loss of soils, as do cities, also.

Cities are located on 11 percent of very good soils of the Earth. Canada is an interesting example. There, cities are liable to obliterate the top quality soils, without any other factor, in this decade; leaving agriculturalists to move on to less sustainable situations. While losing soil, we are calling for at least a sustained productivity, and in some cases an increased productivity, on the soils that remain. As the loss of agricultural soils is largely due to the excess application of energy — mechanical energy, and also chemical energy — then the fact that we are attempting to sustain productivity on the remaining soils, means that the rate of loss must increase, due to the fact that we are using more and more energy on less and less surface.

Let's look now at wind deflation of soils. This has brought about a failing of the inland soils in America. There are soils blowing out to Los Angeles and falling as red rain. Soils from central Australia's marginal areas are falling on the cities as a sort of finely diluted mud, measurable at 12 tons per acre per day. Wind is a major factor in soil loss. The drier it gets, the more wind becomes the factor that we look to. We don't expect to see much agricultural soil by 1990 or 1993; somewhere around there. And there will be a lot of frantic activity on the few remaining patches.

We don't have to look any farther than the soil, or any further than the forest, to see a finite world. I think we can say with confidence that we don't have a sustainable agriculture anywhere in the world, or sustainable forestry.

Water

Even a decade ago, somebody said that water would become the world's rarest mineral. The water table everywhere now is falling rapidly. These are very ancient systems we are playing with. Many of them are about forty thousand years in evolution. No longer is there any way you can get cheap surface water. If you could, Los Angeles would buy it and use it. A major factor in this is the way we seal everything over in cities and highways. We don't get any recharge of soil water. We seal over huge areas with highways. We don't return water to the water table at all. As soon as water is in a river or creek it is gone. It is on its way to the sea, or it is evaporated on the desert salt pan. The flowing river is not really a very useful thing; it is on the way out. There are two very critical areas for water. One is within cities; the other is on the edge of deserts. Both are running into real trouble. Encroaching deserts are killing some millions of people now in Africa. It is visible from the air as mass migrations of herds and people out of the Sahara.

One of the dangers has been the long term disposal of atomic waste in the deep waters. Some of these are beginning to seep through in the Sacramento Valley. You had better start counting the radioactivity coming through in your water supply, or the PCB's, or the dioxin — all of those are in the water table in Maine, New Jersey and California, and, I have an idea, in lots of other places as well. Industry has simply used deep bores to put dangerous wastes into the water table, with the result that large areas of this water table have started to become unviable. I think Boston has ceased to use its ground water. And you'll never be able to use it again. There will be no way you will ever clean that foul water up.

In many towns and cities now, water is running at 700 parts per million dissolved salts, which is at about the limit of the tolerance of the human kidney. At 1,100 parts per million you would experience faintness, accumulation of water in the tissues, all sorts of problems. Most deaths from that commonly occur in the cities, in Perth and Adelaide in Australia, and in Los Angeles in the United States. In all these areas, perhaps, we shouldn't be using water for drinking. It's okay to shower in, although in Atlanta the chlorine alone almost asphyxiates you when you shower. I think about 20 percent of the American males are now sterile by twenty years of age.

Now of course the loss of trees has a pronounced effect on this increased scarcity of water in cycle. . . . I think 97 percent of all water is locked up at all times and only 3 percent goes into any cycling at all, and we are reducing that very rapidly.

At the least we have a desperate future. Our children may never believe that we had surplus food. It is mainly because of utterly ridiculous things. The entire output of atomic power in the United States is exactly equivalent to the requirements of the clothes-drying machines.

"Civilization" To Chaos

Another view of how today's dinosaurs might die comes from Wabun, my longtime friend and co-author. Wabun spent over four months in Peru in late 1989. I feel that her experience there, and the things she observed, will give you a good example of how a civilized country could head toward chaos. As she tells it:

To understand what is happening in Peru, which reflects the situation in much of South America now, it is necessary to know a little about the recent history of the country. Peru, which has about 85 percent Indian or Mestizo people, has been run by European systems since the first Spanish conquest of the Incan people in the mid-1500's. From that time until the last 20 years, Peru was like a feudal society in which the Indians were slaves used for mining, building or agriculture. In this century Peru had a hacienda system in which large Spanish landowners farmed most of the land, using the Indian people as labor. The system was reminiscent of the plantation system in the United States prior to the Civil War.

The Indians lived on the haciendas, worked for the landowners and were given the necessities of life by them, with varying degrees of kindness and fairness. For many years this theoretical republic alternated between military strongmen and fragile civilian governments. In 1968, in a radical break, a communist military dictatorship took power. This government seized all the hacienda land, and made it into cooperative farms with the former laborers now made management. The problem was, the government didn't bother to teach the new managers how to run the farms, so the farms did not produce as they had before. This government was also plagued by economic mismanagement.

In 1980 Peru returned to a civilian government, with a large bureaucracy which is still in place. By the late 1980's, some of the laborers, most often called campesinos, had decided to divide the farms back into private land with each person having their own plot to farm. They did this because under the cooperative system the fruits of everyone's labors were divided equally. That allowed some people to work very little but still have as much as those who worked hard.

While the military dictatorship was in power, it encouraged the campesinos to leave the land and go to the cities. Many did. However, they did not have the skills or knowledge to do well in an urban environment. Today, Peru has a population of about 23

135

million people. As of 1990, about 40 percent live in Lima, the capital city, up 10 percent from a decade ago. Many more live in the smaller cities of Peru. Because of the upsurge in population, there is grinding poverty in these cities.

The migration to the cities was triggered by the clumsy land reform that began in the late 1960's. It now continues because of an unofficial guerrilla war that leaves many people without homes, or safe places to live in the country.

Many urban newcomers live in shantytowns, in homes constructed of straw mats. These new settlements are called "pueblos jovenes," or young towns, by outsiders; "asentamientos humanos," or settlements of humans, by residents. Hunger, crime and disease are rampant in these areas. There is a lot of crime — largely robberies — throughout the country.

The birthrate in Peru is high. Many of the poorer women start having babies at the time of menarche, and don't stop until menopause. Most of these children have little opportunity for education or happiness.

Like many countries in the developing stage, Peru seems to worship the accouterments of the so-called developed nations. Everyone who can get the money to do so buys a car. Most of these cars look like they came from American junkyards. They are driven on the streets as though the drivers were contestants in demolition derbies. Few of the vehicles, even the good ones, have proper exhaust systems so the air is full of noise and automobile emissions.

Peru is in so much debt to the International Monetary Fund that in 1989 the fund threatened to expel them. Most of this is debt run up by former governments for loans that often ended up lining the pockets of government officials. What money Peru doesn't pay to its bureaucracy, it pays to interest on these loans.

The average worker in Peru might make as little as $2 per day, or about $50 per month. In the time I was in Peru, the monetary unit went from 5,000 Intis for $1 U.S. to 15,000 Intis for $1 U.S. Although prices of staples did not climb accordingly, they did climb. There were constant shortages of staple food items like rice, milk, oil and sugar.

Given these economic conditions, it is not surprising that Peru is very willing to exploit, or allow the developed nations to exploit, many of its natural resources. American companies, among others, have large mines in the country. Lumber companies rape the Amazon basin. Commercial fisheries take whatever fish they can, by whatever methods are cheapest for them. If dolphins get caught in tuna nets, few people there are going to complain, given that tuna is one of their important exportable items.

In the pristine Amazon basin and the surrounding mountain areas, the vicunna, a native cousin to the llama, was hunted close to extinction before an international conservation effort saved them. Framed butterflies of incredible beauty are available in all the tourist shops. Anything that people will buy, hungry people will catch and sell. Who cares if a species goes into extinction if it means your children will eat?

Constant Fear

Several terrorist groups add to the general chaos in the country. The one that gets the most publicity is Sendero Luminosa, a Maoist group started by a philosophy professor about 20 years ago. An avowed intention of this group is to bring the country to chaos. That seems a redundant aim given the general conditions in Peru.

The terrorists kill a lot of campesinos, supposedly to terrorize others into joining them. The terrorists are also said to have ties to the "drug lords" who raise cocaine in the mountains of the country. Cocaine is probably the most exportable product — in terms of profit — the country has.

The military also kills campesinos who are suspected of being terrorists. In this regard, the lot of the campesinos is a very difficult one. Their meager living consists of constant fear for their lives and the lives of their children.

In the unofficial guerrilla war that has been taking place in Peru, fifteen thousand people have been killed in nine years. Peru often seems as though it is a society of armed camps.

There is a strong class system in Peru. People of European ancestry, and the few mestizos who have managed to become rich or famous, are at the top of the Peruvian ladder. People who have their own small businesses, or hold administrative or bureaucratic positions, or else have some professional credentials, come next. Then there are the majority of mestizos who are workers in the cities. Beneath them are the campesinos. Most people with money have at least one maid and/or handy-person working for them, for room and board and $10 to $40 per month. I was also struck by the way some people would talk about their servants as though they were sub-humans, incapable of feelings, thoughts or intelligent action.

In talking with people from various classes, I was struck particularly by two things. One was that almost everyone, from every class, agreed that the country was in trouble. (Some people seemed to take pride in the problems in much the same way that well-off Manhattanites talk proudly of their courage in walking the streets or taking the subways.) The other was that most people seemed to be looking for someone to get them out of this trouble, someone other than themselves. There was a sense of helplessness that seemed to affect people from all strata of society. There was also an awareness that those politicians who had promised to get them out of trouble in the past had only increased the country's problems. If it were not for strong family ties, many people in Peru said they would take any chance they could get to live elsewhere.

Fool The Gringo

How did life in the city of Lima seem? There was a constant atmosphere of fear and anxiety. This was exacerbated by terrorist attacks (although few in number), rumors of expected attacks (many in number), and the constant presence of heavily armed public and private police. Every government office was protected by army personnel armed with machine guns. Every bank, and many private stores, employed their own armed private police. Around the time of municipal elections, when terrorists had threatened to mount an offensive, both state and military police cruised parts of the city in vehicles that looked like small tanks or in flatbed trucks with machine guns mounted in all directions.

The fear is also increased by the presence of the poor areas and shantytowns that surround the more prosperous areas of the city. People reported to me that if a well-off person were to walk into these areas, they would not come out alive. While that is probably an overstatement, robberies of all kinds are common throughout the country. Almost every person I talked with who had toured through the country had experienced some form of robbery — anything from having their watch cut off to having their suitcase slit open at the airport.

Peru as a country seems to have an air of desperation. On every street in Lima, for instance, vendors hawk everything from hand-made crafts to balloons, rubber gloves, mufflers and toilet seats. The people selling this wide variety of goods are called "los ambulantes" — the walkers — because they spend their time walking and trying to sell enough so they can eat. Interspersed with the vendors are the "cambistas" — money changers — who are always willing to take dollars and convert them into Intis at whatever the going rate. On the corners of most streets are food sellers, who carry everything from cookies to full meals. To the tourist, all of this makes for an air of exotic excitement. But to the more in-depth observer, it becomes obvious that these people are on the streets selling anything they can in an effort to make enough money to eat.

Beggars are commonplace. Many of them are children dressed in rags who look as though they need a good meal. Yet residents say many of these children are sent out by parents, who take the money and squander it on drink, drugs or gambling.

Other more enterprising young people claim blocks as their territory and "watch" your car if you park it there, protecting it from vandalism, perhaps their own. In exchange, you tip them whatever you wish. Others offer to wash your parked car, again for whatever tip you wish to give. Service-oriented? Picturesque? Yes, but also indicative of the general level of poverty.

Shoe-shine boys abound, waiting to play one of the favorite Peruvian games — "fool the gringo." They offer to shine your shoes for 50¢, then midway through, ask if you want polish of a special kind. If you say yes, they permeate your shoes with something that smells like raw gasoline and then pronounce it a "special shine" that will cost you $3.50.

There is a special gringo price on everything. Usually it is one-third or one-half more than a Peruvian would be charged for the same item or service.

Unfair? In a country where the average worker makes less than $200 U.S. per month, all Americans and Europeans seem rich in comparison.

Underlying the "fool the gringo" mentality is a real mixture of envy and resentment toward the people who are seen both as the cause of the country's problems and, at the same time, the epitome of the people's desires. Everything American — from Reebok sneakers to Cross pens — is highly prized. This love/hate towards Americans is an attitude that some of my other travelling non-Native friends report as being ever more widespread around the world. In most of Central and South America, in Hawaii, in the Caribbean and Pacific Islands, non-Native tourists report feeling ever-increasing hostility from Native people.

An Environmental Disaster

Peru is an environmental disaster. Aside from the cutting of Amazon forest, and the near-extinction of wildlife with any commercial value, there is also a great deal of pollution in Peru. In addition to the emissions from old, badly maintained vehicles, there is industrial chemical pollution. Peru has few, if any, requirements for the dumping of industrial or other wastes. There is also a lot of chemical pollution from household cleaners which are used copiously by the servants and other workers on the orders of their bosses.

While I was in Peru, there was an ad campaign to try to convince people to pick up their garbage from the streets, and to take their garbage bags right to the dump trucks. From the amount of garbage scattered in the streets, this campaign appeared to be meeting with minimal success. The garbage was being scattered by dogs, and also by hungry people who open garbage bags and go through them looking for anything they can eat.

What about the water? Peruvians drink it. Tourists and people rich enough to buy bottled water do not. In an area that almost never gets rain or snow, the life cycle of the water going through the city is almost too frightening to contemplate.

A Peruvian told me that one day in 1989 someone at the water company turned a valve that sent raw sewage rather than clean water through the water pipes of the city, and that people were joking about their friends smelling like sewage. Whether that incident happened through accidental means or was purposeful sabotage, it brought the risk of a full-scale epidemic to the city. What if something like that happened for a longer period? One of the shortages in Peru is of many kinds of medications that are too expensive for the Peruvians to afford. And diseases that are easy to eradicate with medication still exist there. For example, tourists are warned not to buy food from street vendors because many of them carry tuberculosis. Through incidents like these, it's easy to see that the stage is prepared in this country for a raging epidemic that could severely decimate the population.

Two Realities

Some Peruvians told me there are two realities in the country. One is the "official" reality painted by the government and the press. The other is the "actual" reality experienced by the people.

For example, Huancayo is a small city a couple of hours east of Lima. It is reported to be a hotbed of terrorist activity. During the 1989 municipal elections, the government and press said that the city was tranquil during the elections, and that the elections went well. However, people who were there said that no one voted because the terrorists had threatened to cut off the fingers of anyone who did. Besides, they had already assassinated most of the candidates for office. In 1989 alone, 130 Peruvian politicians were killed. Terrorist slogans were all over buildings there, and the sound of bombs exploding was commonplace.

The Future

Peru is an overpopulated country in dire economic straits, with a delicate economic balance and with armed insurgents and armed military ready to do their respective things at the slightest provocation. People are poor and they are desperate.

What would happen if economic conditions worsened? What would happen if the staple food shortages became permanent? In a country of desperately poor, disunited people, hunger alone could send some of them on a rampage that could turn into a full-scale insurrection.

Given all this, what would happen if there were severe natural changes in Peru? What would happen if no rain came to the mountains, the source of the rivers that supply the city? Or if torrential rains came to a city unaccustomed to getting any water? What if a severe cold spell hit a place used to consistently temperate weather? The results of any of these events could be disastrous.

Peru sits on one of the major earthquake faults of the area known as the "Ring of Fire." It has had several large and disastrous earthquakes in the past.

What would happen in Lima or another Peruvian city if a severe earthquake hit? Would people pull together to help each other as some did in San Francisco during the earthquake of 1989? Or would the diverse political elements of the country use the ensuing chaos to create even more problems for the country and its people? Would terrorists use the opportunity to bring the country to its knees? And how would the military respond to any such threat? What would happen when people discovered no food was being shipped from the countryside? Could Peru recover from the economic shock such an event would bring? Or would it deliver an economic and ecological blow from which civilization as Peru knows it now could not recover?

Peru is at this time an extreme example of a country in trouble. But it is not so different from its South and Central American neighbors, or from the countries of Africa and the Orient. And if all of the Third World countries ceased developing as the developed nations have planned, what would happen to the technological giants? Keep in mind that most developed countries depend on developing nations for a lot of their food and raw materials. If these resources were no longer available, how long would it take the technological nations to find themselves in much the same position that Peru is in now?

Bright Day

Chapter Eight

Healing The Earth Now

If you don't like the world you live in, create the world you like — now. Don't wait for the Earth changes to intensify before you start. An important part of the Earth changes is what each human being does now. As a people, we are in the process of opening up spiritually — first comes the spiritual change, then the physical. So, we should be manifesting this change in consciousness by doing powerful things in the world.

Begin by looking at the food you put in your body. You may decide that a jelly roll and a cup of coffee is not the best breakfast. Take a look at the amount of junk food you consume. Think of the cost to the environment in terms of the styrofoam that is used, or the trees that are cut down for throwaway paper wrappings. Think about the air you breathe. It is polluted. Think about the polluted water. Remember that 93 percent of the water on Earth is polluted. Think about the very Earth itself, scarred and polluted. How can you reshape your life to heal these scars? Become a spiritual warrior for the Earth Mother and all your relatives in the creation. Think of things that you can do.

In this chapter I am going to give you some suggestions for helping the Earth and all her children. Because I know it's easy to get depressed by all the sad statistics I gave you in Chapter Four, I have grouped my suggestions in the same categories as the statistics. This way you can see that, even though something like deforestation seems like a monumental problem, you are not powerless in beginning to bring about a solution. Although the Earth changes are already in motion, you do have power to help heal the Earth and yourself. This chapter will help you find out how, both practically and spiritually.

Please pay close attention. At the end of the book, I'm going to ask you to find ways to build upon the suggestions I make in this chapter.

Weather Changes

A lot of people say there is nothing you can do about the weather, but that has not been my experience. While you might not yet know how to be a brother or sister to thunder beings, here are some things you can do.

1. Thank the rain and the snow spirits when they come. Don't tell them they are ruining your day.
2. Call the weather reporters on radio or television who say in the middle of a drought that it's going to be a terrible rainy day or weekend. Tell them that it isn't terrible for the Earth and her people to get the water they need.
3. Respect the sun and your body by limiting exposure. Realize you are getting a lot more than warmth and Vitamin D when you are in the sun these days.
4. Don't plant a nice green lawn if you are in an area where it will have to be watered. Instead, plant native, drought-resistant plants that require little upkeep. If you are in a desert area, enjoy a desert-landscaped yard.
5. If you live in a storm area (coastal or tornado), be prepared for storms that might come. Know what to do. Have the proper emergency equipment. Practice storm drills with your family. Make plans for meeting someplace if you can't get to your house.
6. When traveling, be prepared for unexpected hot and cold weather. Adopt a layered look. Carry along a sun hat and umbrella.
7. Even though it may be extra hot or cold, don't set your thermostat for heat or air conditioning too far up or down. Being energy-efficient during times of weather change will help to reduce further pollution. Try to keep your heat no higher than 65 degrees and your air conditioner no lower than 75 degrees.

Seismic Events

1. Learn about the area where you are living. Is it on an earthquake fault? Have there been quakes in the past?

Is that pretty mountain a dormant volcano?
2. If you are living in an area where seismic events are likely, be prepared. Discuss preparations and various courses of action with family and friends.
3. Learn to listen to the Earth so you will have advance notice if something is going to happen.
4. Make prayers, offerings or ceremonies for the keepers of the fault line or volcano.

Population

I find it hard to believe but there is actually a scientific debate going on about whether there really is a population problem. One side contends having more humans on the Earth is good because it means more brains to think of technological answers to the Earth's problems. I hope the scientists on that side can find a way for the brains not to need food, water and fuel.

1. Limit the number of children you have. If you really love having children, adopt more. There are a lot of "throwaway" children of all varieties in the world today who would just love being with people who would love them.
2. Support education about birth control, both for young people and for people in Third World countries.
3. Support pro-choice politicians in the United States.
4. Support pro-child politicians and legislation so that the young ones coming into the world now have a better chance for a decent life.
5. Support prenatal care for all mothers, and quality preventative medicine for all children in the world.

Water

Here is one problem where each person can make a big difference.

1. Be aware of water usage. Know, for example, that each toilet flush consumes about 5 gallons; each minute of water running in a sink, 3 to 5 gallons; a ten-minute

shower, 50 gallons; each washing machine load, 30 to 50 gallons.

2. Avoid excessive toilet flushing. The rule to follow is, "If it's yellow, let it mellow. If it's brown, flush it down."
3. Many toilets have larger tanks than they need, using more water than is necessary to flush. Put a bottle filled with water or a displacement bag in the tank to save water.
4. Steel sink and bath tub plugs always leak. Get the old-fashioned hard rubber plugs.
5. For your own good, get an effective water filter system. It will filter out a lot of problems.
6. If you use bottled water, buy it in recyclable containers.
7. Adopt a lake, beach or lagoon area and make it your responsibility to maintain its beauty and health. It is sad to see so much water with litter in it.
8. Get a low-flow device for shower, tub and sinks.
9. Use whatever graywater you can. For instance, if you wash your baby with biodegradable soap, you can then use the bath water to do hand wash, and then to water your plants and flowers. Depending on where you live, it might even be feasible to put in a graywater system.
10. Experiment with taking a bath and washing your hair in five gallons of water you heat on the woodstove. The old sponge bath does save a lot of water.
11. Use a basin for washing and rinsing dishes. Doing it under running water is wasteful.
12. Always thank the water spirits for the gift they are giving you.

Agriculture

1. If you celebrate Christmas, don't buy a cut Christmas tree. Get a living one and replant it in your yard or forest. Learn how to care for it. If you are unable to do this yourself for some reason, donate it to a park or forest service organization.

2. Plant a garden. It provides better food for you and enables you to use your compost in a proper manner. Fifty-three percent of households in the United States now garden. They produce 18 percent of the food in the United States.
3. Find ways to raise the yield of your garden. Permaculture, the method developed by Bill Mollison, who was quoted in Chapter Seven, is one good way.
4. Compost all your kitchen food scraps.
5. Make lawn clippings, leaves and woodstove ashes part of your compost.
6. Buy organic foods. Do business with people who are actively trying to show respect for the Earth Mother. Your food money can have a lot of impact on how businesses do things. In California, the organic food industry jumped from a $20 million to a $100 million business in the late 1980's
7. Whenever possible, buy from local farmers. The food will be fresher and therefore healthier, especially since local growers use fewer chemicals than agribusiness. You will also be supporting your local economy.

Forests

1. Plant trees. Buy live Christmas trees and replant them (see #1 under agriculture).
2. Recycle paper.
3. Don't buy things made from tropical hardwoods.
4. Speak out on the deforestation of Brazil and other parts of the world. Remember, it is your world. Remember the number of acres destroyed, and the number of Indian people who have been forced off their land.
5. Tell Brazil that you will not buy their products unless they stop the murder of their Indians, and the destruction of the rain forests.
6. Boycott businesses involved in the destruction of forests anywhere.
7. Let politicians and business leaders know how you feel

about this issue.
8. Pray for the tree spirits.

Nuclear Problems

1. Cut your electricity usage so there is less need for nuclear plants. When people ask me what to do about this problem, I often reply by turning out the light. Remember that the building of new nuclear or coal burning plants is based on the market for energy. It's a supply and demand system. If you ask for more power, electric companies will produce it.
2. If you are building a house, construct it along energy efficient lines, insulate it well, and use solar heat to the extent possible.
3. Let your political representatives know you object to nuclear weapons, nuclear bomb testing and nuclear power plants.
4. Support groups that are bringing the problems of nuclear energy, nuclear bomb testing and radioactive waste to the attention of more people.
5. Pray for peace.

Solar Problems

1. Be aware of the sun, solar storms and solar radiation and their effects upon the Earth.
2. Protect yourself from the dangers that come from solar radiation.
3. Make prayers and offerings to Father Sun, thanking him for all the light and warmth he gives.

The Ozone

Some scientists are now claiming that the hole in the ozone wasn't really caused by chlorofluorocarbons (CFC's) but rather by a volcanic eruption in Antarctica. While volcanos definitely affect the ozone, so do CFC's.

1. Don't use spray containers that have CFC's as propellants.

2. Don't use styrofoam. Carry your own mug with you and use this instead of styrofoam cups. Don't buy products packed in styrofoam.
3. Don't buy halon fire extinguishers.
4. Don't buy clothing that has to be dry-cleaned. Dry cleaning chemicals are harmful to the ozone and toxic in other ways.
5. Don't use your air conditioning unless really necessary. Be sure any air conditioners, particularly automobile types, are running well and not leaking.
6. Have your car's air conditioning system maintained in a shop that recycles CFC's.
7. Keep your car maintained so it doesn't unnecessarily contribute to smog, with its resulting ozone damage. Keep car tires properly inflated; this saves fuel.
8. Use your car less. Carpool, walk. Mexico City has started a program that allows cars with a certain color sticker to drive only on particular days. Promote such a program in your area. Take a bus, train or subway whenever you can.
9. Ride a bicycle. Bicycling and walking both provide good exercise.
10. Visualize the ozone layer whole and complete. Ask the spirit keepers of the ozone to help make this visualization a reality.

Acid Rain

1. See suggestions 7 through 9 in the ozone section. Car emissions contribute heavily to acid rain, as well as to ozone depletion and general smog.
2. Actively boycott companies creating excessive pollution.
3. Use fireplaces only for heat, not for atmosphere.
4. If you heat with wood, use a stove with a secondary burn chamber to get the most efficient use from the wood. Keep the stove and chimney clean.
5. Respect the water cycle by following the suggestions

outlined in the section on water.

Garbage

1. Recycle everything you can. Start a recycling program in your area if one doesn't exist. If one does, use it.
2. Either stop your junk mail or recycle it.
3. Give unused clothes and household items to the thrift store or some person in need.
4. Use old paper to make logs for your fireplace as part of your heating system. Wrap the paper tightly to make the logs. Use paper scraps as kindling.
5. At the Bear Tribe, we keep buckets alongside the toilet and in the outhouses for used toilet paper, which we burn in the woodstove. This helps to keep the septic tank and the latrines from filling up so fast.
6. Remember that newspaper and old telephone books are just fine to use as toilet paper. But don't flush them as they will clog up modern plumbing. Dispose of them in the woodstove or a garbage can.
7. If you have a baby, try to use cloth diapers whenever possible since disposable diapers are a major environmental problem.
8. Don't buy products that have excessive packaging. Buy products in reusable containers.
9. Buy rechargeable batteries.
10. Get good cloth shopping bags that will last for years and use them instead of throwaway plastic or paper bags.
11. If you change the oil in your car yourself, take the used oil to a recycling station. Patronize only those shops which recycle car oil.
12. Keep tires properly inflated so you don't unnecessarily contribute to the 240 to 260 million tires discarded annually in the United States.
13. Take responsibility for the world around you. If you go camping or on a picnic, pick up the litter you see even if it is not yours.

Other Problems

What I am including here are miscellaneous suggestions for dealing with everything not dealt with in other sections.

1. If you smoke for recreation, stop. You are polluting the air not only for yourself, but also for others. If you do smoke, be considerate by picking up your cigarette butts and putting them in the garbage. Remember, they are litter too.

2. If you live in the city and have a house cat, don't let it run free around the neighborhood. Cats can cause great destruction to the birds, rabbits and squirrels, often just killing them for sport and leaving them to rot. If your cat goes out, put a bell on its collar, but in order to protect your cat as well, use a break-away collar.

3. Don't use harsh chemicals and then flush them into the water system. Instead, use biodegradable soap, detergent and cleaning products. Remember that in big cities the water is recycled up to 12 times; then you may be drinking it.

4. Use recycled paper products.

5. Snip plastic six-pack rings so they don't end up killing marine life.

6. Boycott products made from endangered species or products that impose cruelty on animals. Boycott tuna companies whose fishing practices kill dolphins.

7. Keep all your appliances in good shape so they use less energy.

8. There is a good organization in the United States called "Adopt a Highway." Certain local groups take responsibility to pick up all the litter and keep the road clean. Help this program spread.

9. Support the lawmakers who are passing laws to protect the Earth.

10. Stand up against lawmakers who are producing or supporting harmful laws.

11. Speak out and write letters on environmental issues.

Whole societies have changed because people have spoken out.

12. Write letters to the editor on Earth problems. People read them and think.

13. Support projects that help Native people to be self-reliant. There are Native people around the world trying to keep their land and maintain traditional ways. Many Native people are forced to sell all their natural resources just to eat. Or they hunt endangered species for their meat or hides. We could help them create other sources of income.

CAUTION

It takes a while to get all of these ideas working in your life. Be gentle with yourself as you switch to a Bright Day life style. Remember, guilt is a useless emotion. And self-righteousness is, at best, boring. At worst, it creates fascists. Keep a sense of humor. Laughter is the best medicine for you, and your healing helps the Earth also.

Chapter Nine

Practical Preparations For Survival

The Earth changes are coming quickly on all levels of life. In this chapter, I will offer you some practical advice about how to survive them, starting now. Don't wait for the "big one" to get your survival program going. Begin now to develop practical ways to ensure your survival on an everyday basis. Start with the areas in which you feel most comfortable and knowledgeable. Then move on to areas where you will have to stretch a bit to become knowledgeable and competent in taking care of your needs.

A good way to begin is to select one essential for survival — for instance, food — and then spend one day concentrating on all aspects of it as you go through your daily activities. Where do you get your food? How do you store it? How do you cook it? What would you do if your normal routines were interrupted? Could you adapt what you have on hand to meet your needs? How would you do this? Do you need to have more knowledge in this area? Research it now. Do you need different equipment than what you have presently? Purchase it now. If you do all your planning in an orderly manner, it will be a learning experience and can even be fun. But begin now.

Be aware of what you will need in terms of equipment, food, shelter, etc. Project your future needs and purchase items of the best quality. You don't want something cheap and fragile when you may not be able to replace it. If it breaks, you are stuck. Try to learn all of the homesteading skills you can before you need them. Know what is available on the surrounding land. There are still areas where there are a lot of wild foods and fish in the streams. Learn how to dry and can food and how to make jerky.

Another important thing to consider is money. You will want your financial assets to be as liquid as possible, so be very careful about credit. Be aware that all things are subject to change without notice, including the economy. As one old Indian said about the people living in the United States, "How come they got the country for nothing, and now they owe everyone for it?" Those people who have

159

taken out equity loans on their homes might have problems when we have a major economic slowdown. As I've said, economic changes will be part of the Earth changes, and I foresee more people becoming homeless as a result.

We are moving into a time when cash will be king. I feel that you will be able to buy things at times for very little money, if you have cash. And cash will be one of the last things to go out of use. Although gold and silver usually hold their value much longer than anything else, I don't encourage storing them in large amounts because they are cumbersome and hard to convert. Remember also, the search for gold and silver started a lot of the problems we now have on the Earth.

If you have to be in or near a city, be aware of the possibility of earthquakes that will break water mains and gas lines and destroy sewage systems. For the sake of your own survival, know how to shut off your gas, electricity and water. Be sure your home is quake-resistant; have earthquake drills. Major storms also will do great damage; and at a time when no one will be available to repair the damage, that will be it for parts of the country. And be aware that there are enough gas and chemicals stored near every major city to wipe out the whole population of the area. Look at what happened in India from the Union Carbide leak. This kind of disaster can happen anywhere.

If you are in the city, learn how to sprout seeds for food and how to garden indoors. If you have room, plant a garden outside. Find out about buying food from people who raise it near the city. When the trucks aren't running, "truck gardens" could save your life.

Be aware that under stress, crazy people become more crazy. When law and order breaks down, people will become more violent. Crime is increasing in many major cities already. Each year the streets become more unsafe. In the city and suburbs, I always carry a stout walking stick when I walk. This is to fend off wild or mean dogs, or mean humans. You might try to learn the old art of staff

160

fighting, using a long walking stick as a means of self-defense.

When there are no garbage or sanitation services in the big cities, disease and epidemics will spread rapidly. As water and air become even more polluted, just staying alive will become more complicated.

Generally, this is a time to become as mobile as possible. Know the best route out of a city. Have a map of your city that shows alternate streets in case major highways are blocked or the bridges are out. When planning a route out from a major city, take into account the possibility of earthquake damage causing chemical spills, broken gas mains, and downed power lines. Having a full tank of gas in your car at all times will allow you to leave on your own and get as far away from the city as you need to. Remember that gas pumps will not operate if the electricity is out.

If you do have a car, be sure it is in good condition and ready to roll. Good tires, a spare tire or two, tire chains in the northern areas, a jack and wrench to change tires are as essential as is a full tank of gas. If you really want to be prepared, buy a four-wheel drive vehicle. A pick-up with a camper is even better, especially if you carry extra gas cans.

When I travel, I carry with me (even on airplanes) a flashlight, knife, fork and can opener. I was once in Lima, Peru, when terrorists blew up some power lines. I had to walk up to my 11th floor hotel room in the dark. Luckily, I carry a pen light in my pocket at all times. I thank the Great Spirit that this gave me a safe journey.

Another important piece of equipment is a compass, so you will know where you're going, even at night. Learn to read a compass and a map.

Try to prepare to survive as comfortably as possible. One of the things that I encourage people to do is make any life style comfortable. For instance, if you are starting out with a tent, put it up in a place that has the least bugs

161

and provides the most comfortable place to camp and sleep. There is no reward for making life harder.

Remember that smaller towns are safer than big cities. Of course, living in the country is even better than being really prepared in the city or a small town, especially if you have water, your own source of fuel, and land that can produce food.

Learn about an area before you go into it. In some of the southern areas of the United States, as well as elsewhere, there are a lot of bug problems. You don't want to go into places where you can be eaten up by mosquitoes, ants or ticks. Be aware that ticks in many parts of the United States transmit Lyme disease or Rocky Mountain Spotted Fever. Be aware of these kinds of problems so that you can take care of yourself.

Once you have made up your mind about where you want to live in the country, learn about the surrounding area. Learn about the wild edibles and how to correctly harvest them so you do not decimate them in one year. Learn how to forage and harvest crops that would otherwise go to waste, such as fruit in abandoned orchards. Where there is wild game in the area, understand their habits and how to hunt in a conservative manner. Have the equipment that you will need if you have to hunt.

In choosing your homesite, remember that electricity may not be available after a period of time. You may well be dependent upon sunlight and candles. Look carefully for all of the things you might need. Water in many areas may be contaminated. Strengthen your knowledge and skills about finding and purifying water. Spend time researching. Otherwise those things you don't understand could result in your death, because of fear or because you are unprepared. People really have died in the desert and in the mountains just wandering around in circles, unprepared and afraid. Know the essentials you will need and take them into account before you need them. The better prepared you are, the more chance you and the people with you will have of surviving. Find out if anyone in your area has medical skills, and learn as much first aid as possible yourself. Keep a basic first aid kit in both your home and your car.

Wherever you live, if you have a fireplace or wood stove in your house, thank the Great Spirit because I see power failures and natural gas shortages occurring. Save all scrap paper and use it for your fires; newspaper can be rolled into logs for the fireplace. Get yourself a chain saw and learn how to use it. Also, a skill saw is good for cutting up small boards and tree limbs. I once cut our supply of wood for the whole winter with a skill saw. Always keep as much wood as possible on hand and store it where it will stay dry. Trying to burn wet wood is a real problem.

Throughout the time of the Earth changes, we are going to have to make an extra effort to take more responsibility for our health and well-being, because a lot of the things we might need on a personal basis may not be available. Something that I encourage everyone to do at this time is to get any special medical treatment that is needed or that requires special equipment or medication. For example: buy an extra pair of glasses; have dental work done; get any surgery that you feel you might need. Do these kinds of things now because, as the Earth changes progress, they won't be so readily available. And sometimes it's the small things that can knock you off balance.

Try to keep your body in as good a condition as possible. I walk and do light yoga to keep in shape. Wood splitting and gardening are good, useful ways of working out also. I was 61 years old on August 31, 1990, and I feel I'm in reasonably good shape. I have my little aches and pains, but overall, my body works well — Thank You Great Spirit!

Always keep in the trunk of your car basic survival equipment, a sleeping bag, and one gallon of water. In the house, store at least five gallons of drinking water and keep it fresh (do the same for the gallon in your car).

In many places in the United States now, you need a water filter system because otherwise the water is unsafe to drink. The same is true in Germany and most other parts of the world. In one instance recently, the mother of one of my apprentices took sick in Cincinnati, Ohio. She had a constant upset stomach and loose bowels. After much testing, the cause was determined to be the city water.

I strongly urge you to learn proper food storage techniques and to have on hand at least a five-day supply of dried food or fruit and nuts. Use this up and replace it about every five months so you always have fresh food.

For your future diet I suggest a diet with a lot of grains, beans and lentils. If you move toward this now, you will be a lot healthier and so will the planet. If you buy your food in bulk, there is less transportation cost and almost no packaging, so less trash, and you are getting better food. The best plan is to project your food needs for one to three years. Remember, food is one of the best investments you can make. It is always going up in price, so there is good interest on your investment.

Here are some helpful tips for using your grains and beans. Wheat can be soaked and sprouted, and sprouted wheat bread is super to eat. Alfalfa can be sprouted or planted for greens to cook, use in salad or make tea. I always soak beans and peas overnight, so it takes less energy to cook them. Get a good grain grinder — one that will work by hand. Electric grinders are available although you can crack wheat in your blender until you have to resort to a hand grinder. Whole wheat can be soaked and cooked for breakfast. There is lots of energy and nutrition in it. Keep salt (for preserving and flavoring) and cayenne pepper (to warm the body in cold weather) in your reserve, as well as other herbs for seasoning.

Then, if you have a small garden space to raise some vegetables, you're set. You will be able to eat and provide for yourself and your loved ones, and you will be helping the planet by no longer adding packaging garbage to the

Earth.

There are people who have lived in tents for many years. If you are going to buy a tent, be sure it is really waterproof. Get a well-insulated sleeping bag. That will be a good investment. Be aware that down-filled gear will not keep you warm if it gets wet, so look for other options.

You should have a good backpack and water canteen in case you have to leave an area on foot. Your backpack should be big enough to carry your needs, yet small enough so you can actually carry it. Get a good backpack that's strong and comfortable. Don't try to pack more weight than you can handle. In your backpack should be extra socks, matches, water purification tablets and a five-day supply of food. Good socks and shoes are important; blistered feet don't walk very far. Foods I recommend include dried fruit, nuts, trail mix and easily prepared survival foods. Rotate these and test them out. Also have a compass and any maps you need. With these on your back you can leave a disaster area on foot if need be.

Following is my long-term survival list (not necessarily in order of importance). This is what I feel is required in order to make a planned move, not one made out of panic. It also includes items you'll need if you are planning to stay in the country for the duration of the changes. Understand that in all instances you are making preparations necessary for your long-term survival.

1. Water stored to last at least 5 days, at one gallon per day per person.
2. A good canteen and basins to catch rainwater in. Also have a good supply of water purification tablets or bleach, or plan to boil your water. The surest way to purify water is to boil it for 15 to 20 minutes. If you have a good stream or spring say, "Thank you Great Spirit."

3. Below is a suggested list of what would be basic food items for long-term survival. This list is per person, for one year.

> Wheat, 300 lbs
> Rice, 100 lbs
> Beans, Peas, Lentils, 50 lbs *each*
> Honey or Sugar, 60 lbs
> Salt, 3 lbs
> Cayenne Pepper, 1 large can
> Herbal Seasonings
> Dried Milk, 80 lbs
> Peanut Butter, 50 lbs
> Dried Fruit
> Canned food, or dried (ready to mix) food
> Oatmeal, 50 lbs
> Alfalfa Seeds, 10 lbs
> Sardines, optional (but my favorite)

If you have a baby, include formula and baby food. If you have pets, you will want food for them as well. Your food needs to be stored in waterproof containers, capable of also protecting against insects and mice. I prefer steel garbage cans or plastic five-gallon buckets. The vacuum sealed method is also very good. If you are storing nuts or oatmeal, they smell and taste bad after a while, so they will need to be rotated. For all storing of food the rule is: use up the old and replace with the new.

4. Manual grain grinder.

5. Medicines. Assemble a standard first aid kit, with a comprehensive first aid book. But also include things for headaches, upset stomach, congestion, colds and wounds; disinfectants; prescription medicines; and anything else you use regularly. My own medical survival kit also includes vitamins (good multi-vitamins, B complex and vitamin C), apple cider vinegar, honey, garlic, sage tea for colds, mint tea, golden seal, brandy (good as medicine and on cold nights), herbal

tinctures, hops, catnip (which helps you sleep), herbs for cooking, including dried garlic and onions, cayenne pepper, cumin, basil and coriander and don't forget salt. After you've been eating rice and beans for a few days, they'll need lots of help to make them taste good.

6. Toothbrush, baking soda or salt to brush with, a good supply of dental floss (a multi-use item) and any other items you need for good tooth care.

7. Extra glasses.

8. For a camp kitchen you need: camp stove with good supply of fuel (in wooded areas, all you need are rocks and a flat tin or grill), pots and pans, plates and bowls (unbreakable — Army surplus camp kits serve very well), cooking utensils, knife, fork, spoon, spatula, biodegradable dish soap, towels, bucket to carry water, dish pan, matches dipped in wax and stored in waterproof containers.

9. A good tent, sleeping bags for each person, extra blankets, sleeping pads, and ground cloth — and another waterproof tarp to cover your camp gear.

10. Clothing. Have clothing for all weather. Include a good warm coat and sweaters, rain gear, a good pair of hiking boots that will take years to wear out, warm winter underwear, wool socks, summer socks (a lot of people have been hurt by blisters on their feet from socks with holes in them — learn to darn or mend socks), work gloves, hats, and whatever else you need for warmth and protection.

11. Hunting equipment. There might be situations during the changes in which hunting will be necessary for survival. If that is the case, you should be prepared both with equipment and knowledge of how to use it. My choice, if I were to have only one gun, would be a .22 caliber rifle because I am a fair marksman. I can kill everything up to a deer with it. Purchase 500 rounds of .22 hollow point bullets.

   If you are not an experienced marksman or may be

depending on deer and elk or other large animals for survival, then get a 30-30 or 30-06 and at least 200 shells. A shotgun comes in handy for shooting things flying or running.

But the bow and arrow is still one of the best weapons. With it, you are part of the whole action. When you get good at it, you can provide for your needs and not have to worry about running out of shells. Plus, there is no noise pollution. You may want to be unheard, and unseen, as you may need to survive where there are unfriendly people.

12. Fishing. Get yourself some basic equipment. Include assorted sized hooks, fishlines, sinkers, etc. Fishing takes time. But if you are moving toward long-term survival, time is something you will have plenty of.

13. Wood stove. One with a secondary burn chamber uses less wood, creates less pollution. Select a model with top-surface space to cook on.

14. Chain saw, and extra gas and oil, spark plugs, chain, etc.

15. Bow saw and a tool to set the teeth with, extra blades.

16. Skill saw (for when you have electricity).

17. Axe, hatchet, files.

18. Splitting maul.

19. Flashlights with extra batteries and bulbs; candles; propane, kerosene, or Coleman lantern with plenty of fuel, and extra wicks and mantles.

20. A good pocket knife; a sharpening stone.

21. Hammers, assorted nails, assorted screws, wrench set, pliers, wire cutters, screw drivers, pipe wrench, 200 feet of one-quarter inch nylon rope, duct tape.

22. Shovels, spades, hoes, and rakes with strong teeth.

23. Charging system — wind, water or solar — to pump water and provide electricity.

24. Backpack. It should have numerous compartments and should be waterproof. Your backpack is essential for your survival. If you are forced to relocate, it may be

all that goes with you.

25. Compass.
26. Up-to-date topographical maps of the areas you want to live in. These can show you land and water away from human habitation.
27. A 4-wheel drive vehicle with all the proper tools needed for maintaining it.
28. Tire chains.
29. Radio. Have two: one, electrically operated and the other, battery or solar powered. You'll want to know how the Earth changes are coming along.
30. Soap for laundry and bathing (when you run out, learn to make your own).
31. Natural insect repellent.
32. A mirror, so you can see yourself once in a while. It is also good for flashing signals.
33. By this time, you should have replaced toilet paper with newspapers and old telephone directories.
34. Female needs. (My mother used cloth pads which she washed.)
35. Baby diapers. Kids can go bare-bottom in the summer — and some do in the winter. If yours don't, you should be using cloth diapers. You can convert later, if need be, to moss or dry grass. The Chippewas once used what they called a "moss bag" made of buckskin. The moss was changed when necessary.
36. The good books you always wanted time to read.

Because it is sometimes hard to find the time to locate all of the supplies needed for survival, a friend of mine is preparing survival kits, and offers grains, beans, lentils, and other dried foods in bulk quantities. He also sells a wide variety of other things helpful for long-term survival, all based upon the ideas I've presented in this chapter. For more information, see Randy Tiger Food Distributors in the resource section at the end of the book.

Chapter Ten

Attitudes For Survival

One of the major things required of Bright Day people is a consciousness different from that of society-at-large. Foremost in this consciousness is an awareness of the Earth. When I first began teaching and travelling around to share knowledge with other people, Spirit told me that I should only share with those people who were ready, who were open and willing to learn. I was told to go only where I was invited. I was instructed to teach those who were seeking knowledge in a sacred manner, who really loved the Earth enough to look for a balance and harmony with the planet and the rest of creation. I was told to work only with people who were not destructive or war-like. I was told to seek people who did not have arrogance in their personalities. Rather, they should have the capacity to understand the basic Native teaching that we should blend with the Earth, not try to conquer it.

The Earth cleansing is also a time of cleansing for human beings. It's a time for human beings to sort out the past belief systems that helped create the world we see around us. What we have now is a world of destruction — of the planet and of many of our fellow beings. So people need to free themselves from a lot of preconceived ideas that put them into conflict with nature, that give them the idea they are superior and have the right to destroy anything around them.

These past belief systems told people the Earth was only a temporary resting place. They taught people they were going to go up to heaven so they didn't have to take responsibility down here for the planet. As a result of these concepts, people have caused a lot of destruction on the Earth. Now people need to take a look at their thoughts and ideas and what they have created.

This is the time for human beings to start creating a new belief system, one based on the truths that are evident in nature. All people who wish to survive have to start learning some of the things that Native people know about being in harmony and balance with life around them.

171

I feel — and Spirit has told me also — that this is a time for human beings to find the spiritual beliefs that link them to the Earth. This is a time to seek power spots and find places to pray and reconnect with the natural forces and with the spirit helpers that have been upon this planet for thousands of years. Through this praying and seeking, people also will learn how to show love for their fellow human beings. They will learn to come back into the balance that is necessary for their survival and for the survival of the planet.

I'm told by Spirit that we have to build a belief system in which we carry the law in our hearts — not one where we look over our shoulder to somebody else. We have to learn to take direct responsibility for our lives on an everyday basis. This is one of the things I've tried to impart to people through my teachings and writings. This is part of what I see as my work.

I find that there is a great hunger in people to find out about ways in which to heal themselves; first themselves, you see, then they can really help others and the Earth. That's why I stress the need for every person to take real responsibility for their own life. I feel that everyone has the right to speak to the Creator, to discover and follow their own vision.

One of the things that keeps people from their path is money. They think they have to make more and more all the time. And they can always give a good reason — maybe their house is going to cost more this year, or they want to have a car like Joe's down the street, or they need to get new clothes, take a vacation or send the kids to college.

My older brothers and I lived on 80 acres in northern Minnesota, and we supplied all the food we needed. We enjoyed a complete cycle of life between what we'd gather, hunt and fish and what we harvested. Our cycle went along fine until my older brothers had to leave because their "want-to's" got in their way. They wanted to have something else. They wanted to drive a new car, they wanted to do this and that. So, they started moving out. As they wanted more things, they had to make more money. They ended up in the big cities to get that money they needed.

Sometimes you need someone to press your buttons to make you think a little bit. If you're stuck on the little treadmill of always having to make more money, you're paying for it in lots of ways. You're paying for it with your guts.

The Forbidden Energy

You need to look at what this society has done to people over the years to create the problems and the "want-to's" we have today. I've told you how, back in Europe when this current historical era began, they neutered people and took away their feelings of their own male/female energy and replaced it with "no-no's." They put people into little boxes where they couldn't be natural anymore. The Native people call this "forbidden" energy the "life force." The Huichols in Mexico call it *Kupuri*. This energy flows through all of us all the time. It makes the grass grow, it makes you grow, it makes *all* things grow.

One of the most powerful Native ceremonies that we do is at the time of Earth Renewal. This is the time when we celebrate the return of Father Sun — the Winter Solstice — that begins our ceremonial year. During the Earth Renewal, all fires are put to sleep. Then we usually start our sweatlodge fire first, lighting it in the old way with a twirling stick, or flint and steel. Then we make prayers as we start the other fires of our lodges from this first fire.

That first fire, that kindling of light, represents the return of Father Sun. When Father Sun returns and brings his blessing upon the Earth Mother, life is renewed. The growth cycle is renewed for another year. It's a very sacred thing because if Father Sun doesn't return, we're all out of business.

Down in the southwestern United States, the Native peoples in the Pueblo area of the Hopi country watch the

173

"Sunwatcher Peaks" in Arizona. By the shadow of these two peaks, they can tell when the sun has moved farthest south. When it does, they start the celebrations to welcome back Father Sun. The blending of the Father Sun and the Earth Mother — the male and the female energies coming together — brings forth new life.

I try to teach my apprentices that the life force, that surging male/female energy that we feel in us, is real power. If a man and woman make love at the right time of the month, they can bring forth new life. That same energy can be used in many other ways, such as healing. When we learn how to work with the life force on an everyday basis, we can project it outward as a living force of power.

Some people get a little nervous around me because I have a lot of male energy and Earth energy. People can feel that energy and they say, "Hey, that's alive, there's something alive there." Every time the Earth is surging, I feel that power, that whole creative life force surging up in me. Sometimes I have to pull myself down on the ground because I'm feeling my whole power coming through, and I need to ground it in the Earth.

We should be able to learn how to use that energy as a living force in our everyday life. We need to feel it and not have guilt trips over it.

When I embrace a woman, I feel that surging energy and it feels good. Maybe somebody's looking over my shoulder and saying, "Ah, look at that old Sun Bear, that horny old Sun Bear over there." They get worried about it. But I ask, "Creator, who put this in me to make me feel this good energy when I embrace like this? Oh, you did. So, it's okay then." If anybody has problems with my embracing women, they'd better check their own attitude, because I'm not bothered by it.

When you begin to question something, instead of accepting the crap that has been taught to you, you have to be brave. But you do have to start questioning the source of the trips that society has put on you. Otherwise, societal messages are going to keep you locked in your little boxes until the Earth changes shake you out of them.

The dominant society forces people to wear masks. When they get up in the morning, they have to put on a mask before they go to the office. Then they have to put on a mask for their family because their relatives don't quite understand what they're doing, or what they really want to be. They put on a mask when they go to church, and maybe they even wear a mask for their own mate. By the time they get done wearing all these masks, they no longer know who they are. This is the way the system keeps people dancing to its tune.

I look at these problems, and I have to make a total indictment of the whole system because it has created all these habits in people. Sometimes I feel very sad when I look around; I don't know how some of these poor babies even make it through life when they just accept all this without question.

Society gives you all these guilt trips and assigns you all these different numbers. So I'm very glad I walk the sacred path. I haven't allowed people to put their guilt trips on me, too much. I just don't allow them to. If they try, I walk away and say, "Hey, I know who I am. This is what I believe and this is what I practice."

I look at all the emotional cripples this society has made. Psychiatry is one of the fastest growing professions in this country, because people need psychiatrists — they really need them. One out of three people in this country has severe mental or emotional problems. We often don't see how bad some of these problems are until someone gets a gun in their hands and kills five or ten innocent bystanders.

Such people get their rubberbands wound too tight, and all of a sudden, they break. There are a lot of suicides right now, and people kill themselves in a lot of different ways, too. Blowing their heads off isn't the only way they do it. There are big question marks in many accidents. How many automobile *accident* deaths, for instance, are actually suicides? A person who is unhappy in life just may decide to turn their vehicle out in front of a big truck. This kind of thing happens all the time.

Palace Or Tomb?

The isolation which pervades this society has caused us some pretty severe problems. There are a lot of deep psychological and emotional problems in society because of loneliness — the greatest sickness society has. People are crying because they are alone. Yet, they're afraid to reach out to someone; they don't know how to reach out any-more. They've locked themselves into their tight little boxes. I look at it, and I feel sad sometimes.

Not long ago, I went to Vancouver, British Columbia. Vancouver is a nice, big city. It's very interesting to watch people in cities everywhere because they are always moving from one box to another. The amount of money you have determines how big your box is. Consequently, some of the boxes are getting pretty small. I looked at some of my friends' apartments and condos in Vancouver, and I said, "Well, life is getting more simple for you guys. When you die, all they'll have to do is slide a concrete slab over the door. You're already in your tomb."

I don't want to see you pushing your belongings out of the cities on little pushcarts when the changes increase because you didn't get the word when your mother, the Earth, was telling you it was time to pack. That's why I'm communicating with you now. The Spirit told me to take the information I have and tell it straight. It's time to stop and say, "Hey, maybe I'd better check my attitudes." The Creator doesn't want people coming into the next world carrying the same worn ideas that are so against life.

It's very important that you look carefully at who your prison-keepers are. There are any number of people — business and industry leaders, advertising executives, clergy and politicians — who have been lying to you and telling you that it's for your own good. As I said, this is a time when a lot of things are being uncovered, and I think that's really good. A lot of people who aren't honest about what life means and what we're here for are getting into trouble right now. Their problems are going to multiply.

From now until the year 2000, there are going to be a lot of things happening. A lot of people are going to be leaving this world — dying off in various ways. To survive, you'll have to walk past the traumatic events taking place around you. You'll have to have a balance within yourself that will enable you to look at these things in a way that won't overwhelm you. You'll need to be able to look at these events and say, "This is what's happening." And then accept the reality of it and move on.

Picking Causes Pain

We can help heal the world by easing tension instead of aggravating it. In relationships and families in this society, we have a problem with tension points. Sometimes there's a little thing, a rub, between two people, and instead of being aware of it and easing off, some people seem to like to pick at it. That's what causes a lot of the pain in the world. If somebody is sensitive about a certain subject, maybe you don't need to rub their nose in it. You can help that person without pounding them into the ground.

If I feel something is helpful to a person, I'll see how much of it they're willing to talk about. But I don't wear them out with it. It's very important to understand that when you're dealing with human beings.

One of the first things people need to do to ease their tension is to get rid of their "garbage." Many Native people have very old practices for doing this. When I was in the Mayan country, the Mayans showed me how they have people get rid of their garbage — the mental and emotional problems they carry in their heads, their anger, fear, and jealousy. The Mayans have a person walk into a stream of moving water and say all the things they feel badly about.

The person speaks the "garbage" into the water, and the water carries it away. This is how the Mayans get rid of their negativity.

Other Mexican Indians have another powerful method. They build a statue of a man out of papier-mâché, which they call "Dr. Gloom," and then they write any problems they have on pieces of paper and put them on the statue. After they have put all the pieces of paper on the statue, they burn it. All their negative feelings go up in smoke.

The ancient Jewish people used a goat for this purpose. In the spring they would put a goat in the middle of a circle and then gather and pray over it. Then they would tell the goat the things they had done that year that they felt badly about. After these confessions had been spoken "into" the goat, the priests would lead it out into the wilderness. The Jewish people called this goat the "scapegoat" — that's how the word entered the English language. The scapegoat went away and took all of the people's guilt along.

Other tribal peoples have other ways to get rid of negativity. Some Southwest Indians have a ceremony where people dance through the village with swords, driving out all the negative spirits. Afterwards, people come through and brush away anything else that's left behind with brooms made from cedar branches. Then they do a blessing with sacred cornmeal.

In my tribe, the Chippewa people, we would have a person go out onto the land and dig a hole. Then they would speak into the hole all of the things they felt badly about — anything that was bothering them or giving them problems. Then they would cover the hole and pray that the problems would remain there, that what was said would be transformed into fertilizer for the Earth Mother. Sometimes we'd give the person a seed to put into the hole so they could see the good growing from the release of their negativity.

It's very important to dump out negativity, that residue of ill-feeling you carry around. I've had people come to me with a lot of anger inside them. A woman who believed she had cancer came to me for a healing. After I'd done the healing, the pain went away and she felt better, but I told her she had another problem.

"You have a deeper problem that's causing this," I said. "You have something much deeper. You hate somebody a lot."

"Yes, my ex-husband," she said. "Every time I hear his name, I go into a rage."

I said, "That's where your sickness is coming from. That's what's eating at you; that's what's eating you away. You're going to have to get rid of that." She lived near Mill Valley, California, and I told her, "You dig a hole in the ground and you dump all your garbage and all your anger into that hole. Keep digging holes until you've gotten rid of it. I don't care if you have to dig holes all over Mill Valley."

I saw her about a month and a half later. She came to a workshop that I was doing and said, "I feel so much better, Sun Bear. I've gotten rid of it. I had to dig a lot of holes, and I might have to dig a few more, but that's the best thing that's ever happened to me!"

I've worked with many different people, including psychiatrists and other professionals, and many of them have found digging a hole to be a good way to get rid of negativity, anger, and fear. These things are keeping you from becoming a whole, balanced, beautiful human being. They are taking power from you. The whole time you're blocking yourself up with these kinds of feelings, you're keeping yourself from getting the good knowledge, energy and support that comes from the creation.

It's your responsibility to release this negativity because it's your garbage. You've got to accept responsibility for it, and for getting rid of it so you can have space in your head for the Creator to give you new teachings. It's very important to understand this and be willing to release your negativity in a real way. A lot of people reach a point where negative thoughts are the only things in their heads. Then they really think they need them. Digging holes is a very effective way of getting past that stage.

Death Or Paradise?

As far as I'm concerned, the Creator put us here on the Earth knowing exactly what we are about, how we function, what we feel, how we experience, and everything. I don't feel that we were put here to make the Earth Mother a prison colony. I think we're placed here to grow to our fullest potential as human beings. We are here to grow.

All the possibilities of life are before us — that's the interesting part of the dance. The Creator throws all the possibilities into the center of the circle and says, "Okay, kids, here it is. You have all these things to work with, and you can either blow each other's heads off or you can create a paradise. It's all up to you."

Sometimes it looks like there are a lot more people wanting to blow each other's heads off than to live in a positive manner. We are at the time right now when we have to look at all the attitudes we've been conditioned to believe. There's no longer any escape from their consequences; we have to look at what we've created.

Recently somebody asked me, "Sun Bear, what do you fear most in the world?" "Not the atomic bomb," I said. "What I fear more than anything else in the world is human conditioning. I fear the little thinking caps which have been clamped on people's heads to get them to accept a certain belief system."

This conditioning exists all over the world. In Iran, Mr. Khomeini took over and set up a system where he controlled some people's minds completely. He told his young people, "You go across the mine field there, and Allah is waiting on the other side for you." His own warped mind built that conditioning. And then thousands — it would have been millions if he could have had his way — marched

180

to be slaughtered. This contemptible bastard had no respect for any human being, the Earth or anything else.

The people you have to watch most in the world are the extreme moralists — *remember that*. They are the most dangerous. And you've got to watch them because they are very dogmatic. Adolf Hitler was an extreme moralist. So was Khomeini. There are also a number of them in the clergy.

I need to tell you that there are also extreme moralists in the New Age field. Some of them have one little idea about diet or something else, and they're ready to sentence you to death if you don't do it their way.

Growth Of Freedom

When you become locked into your little box, you might as well turn in the key and forget it because you're on the way to the cemetery. There's no more growth for you. To keep growing you have to maintain flexibility in your mind.

I feel fortunate that I went to school only through the 8th grade. I realize now what I escaped from. At one point I felt bad because I had only an 8th grade education, but later I found out that what I did not learn has put me in a position to move with greater mobility than most people. I have authored seven books; five of them with a co-author. I'm in the process of working on more books and I've also been the publisher of a major magazine for over 20 years. I travel all over the world most of the year to lecture and teach.

Over the years I've also been involved in developing different projects and small industries, working with many different kinds of people along the way. I've also been involved in economic development for Indian reservations. So, now I'm glad I never went further in school, because I might have ended up learning I needed a "degree" to do something constructive with my life.

The only time I've been to college has been to teach. I taught journalism and Native American Philosophy at the

University of California at Davis for a while. One person in the Philosophy Department was afraid I would get tenure in the university system of California with only an 8th grade education, so she successfully arranged to kick me out. But I came back in through another door — the Experimental College — and taught some more.

While I was teaching at the Experimental College, young people would come up to me and tell me they'd be going to school for four years. I'd say, "What are you going to school for?"

"So I can get a job," they'd reply.

I'd look at them and say, "If you learn anything in your four years, you'll know you don't need a job."

I don't need a "job" now. I've learned how to create my own because I got tired of performing the little dances for others, asking other people for permission to be.

Taking power over your life in such ways is part of the growth of freedom. We are in a time when all my brothers and sisters have to become free — free from whatever you're allowing to hold you back.

Some of you are going to get mad when you begin to realize what's happened in your lives. Men and women come to me for consultations, and they get very angry when they start to look at their lives from my perspective. They often come to realize that somebody has stolen their life. That somebody can be a man, a woman, an uncle, an aunt, a member of the clergy, or a politician. It's somebody they have allowed to steal seven years, ten years, or twenty years of their life by telling them what to do. These men and women were afraid to follow their own convictions. They say, "Well, I would have done this, or that, but my uncle wouldn't let me, my husband wouldn't let me, my wife wouldn't let me."

When we don't live our own lives and become whole human beings, we look for people to blame it on. It's really sad. Part of getting your power in a sacred manner requires breaking free from your prison-keepers, and understanding that what the society that produced the prison-keepers has done to you, it's also done to the Earth, the Sacred Mother. You're going to have to break free, because if you have little shackles on you, it's really hard to help yourself, much less anybody else. You can't become a spiritual warrior when you have shackles on and somebody else is calling the shots.

Some people wonder about me because I walk my path in the sacred manner and because I have been doing this for a long time. Once, however, when I was quite young, I married a lady who was becoming a lawyer. She became a lawyer and divorced me — I think it was her first case!

After that divorce, I decided I would not need to have somebody say words over me to tell me who I could be with in the land that belonged to my ancestors. I decided marriage was something that was only between a man and a woman, based on what was in their hearts. So I never got "married" again. But today I share my life with Jaya, the wonderful woman to whom this book is dedicated.

Also, I have two daughters from earlier relationships. Their mothers went on to other things, and I feel good because they found what they needed to do in life. Knowing them both has been a very good experience.

When I parted ways with Betty, the mother of my oldest daughter, we were dividing up the different things in the household, and I said, "Okay, honey, you take the furniture because you're moving to a new place." I helped her move the furniture into the apartment she was renting. I also said, "Well, you take the cat," since I didn't know if I'd have a place for a cat. We had some savings from living on my money and putting her teacher's salary into a savings account. I was eventually going to a reservation to work with the people there, so I wouldn't have any need for it. I told Betty to take the bank account and I would work the rest of it out from there. Betty took all these different things, and everything worked out fine between us.

Finally, all that was left was a bowl with two goldfish

in it. I looked at them and decided that they represented Betty and myself. "Well," I told the fish, "we're going into another bigger world, and you deserve the same." So I took the goldfish to a pond on Third Street in Los Angeles, put them into the water and said a prayer over them. I wished them well and said, "You grow in the sacred manner." That was my ceremony; that was my divorce!

Power Is Responsibility

Learning to take power over your life in a sacred manner means learning to take responsibility for your actions. And that means breaking free from the habit of saying that somebody else is responsible for you. We have a lot of ways of shirking responsibility; one of the most interesting is how we make someone or something else responsible for the terrible things that come into our lives. Our conditioning determines how we do this.

For instance, if something goes wrong in the life of a Judeo-Christian, that person says, "Well, the devil made me do it." One guy I know was involved in a stock market fraud in Spokane, Washington. He became a born-again Christian, and then he said, "Jesus saved me." He told the judge he was going to become a good Christian so the devil wouldn't make him do any other bad things.

The New Age people have their own ways of shirking responsibility. When their lives don't work for them, they sometimes come to me and say, "My life is a mess. Be my teacher and fix it for me, Sun Bear," or "Tell me how I created this reality."

"Well, it's your mess," I tell them. "You fix it. And it's your reality. Understand it."

A New Age fellow was driving a car that ran out of gas on our way to an airport. I had been looking at the needle since we got into the car because there hadn't been much gas to start with, but when the car stopped he said, "Well, that happened because I have bad karma."

I said, "Hey, put a little good karma on your breakfast

food in the morning — that ought to do it. The reason this happened is because you didn't put gas in the car!" My best reply to "karma" is a bumper sticker I saw which read, "Shit Happens."

Native American people also have ways of shirking responsibility. A Native man and I were going to a pow wow when he had a flat tire. This old tire looked like it should have been junked 5,000 miles ago. It didn't have any tread left on it at all, and there was a big hole through it. The guy told me, "Well, I had a flat tire because somebody put bad medicine on me."

I said, "No, that's not it, brother. Look at that tire. It's worn out. You had a flat tire because you were too stupid to change it!"

It's necessary for us to look clearly at how we have created the world we live in. Whenever I visit any place in the world, I'm always asking, "Who made these people?" I'm not asking who their parents are; I'm asking why these people have become *the way they are*. Who has molded these people? Who has shaped their patterns of thinking in a particular way? That's what I'm interested in.

You need to look at these things, even though sometimes, when you start peeling the layers off, it might be a little painful. You may have to look at some of your sacred cows. You may have to look at some bad things that people have done to you for a long time while telling you it's for your own good. It may be a little shattering to find out just how many sneaky dances society has used to play with your head, to make you accept the patterns of life you're in. Although it may be painful, it is necessary to look.

What you must be able to do in life to be ready for the Bright Day is to sort things out and create a philosophy. I tell people the only philosophy I ever want to hear about is one that will grow corn. This means that the philosophy has to work here and now *every day* of your life on Mother Earth. You shouldn't have to wait until you get to heaven for it to work for you. If something is not real now, if it's not working now, get it out of your life. If your philosophy is not helping you walk in a sacred manner, and giving you the backup power that you need for your survival on the planet now, then you'd better recheck your circuits.

Walking on the sacred path enables you to get all of the things in your life going in the same direction, so you don't have to apologize for any part of your life. You shouldn't have to hide any of your life over in a little corner and be afraid that people will see it.

Get to the point where you don't have to answer to somebody else for your life, where you don't have to be explaining yourself to other people. Otherwise, you're going to be loaded down with a lot of phony guilt. Guilt is a totally useless emotion. It wastes energy. It takes energy from you and keeps you from growing, from becoming a whole human being. Get rid of it.

Don't wait for "something to happen." Start learning to get yourself in balance and move in a sacred manner now. Learn how to will things into existence. Learn how to make things happen. That's part of becoming a spiritual warrior. When you're in there and you're doing your very best in a sacred way, then it's time for you to start calling on the spirits to help you with the rest of it.

We are, right now, at a time that my Kahuna brothers and sisters speak of: a time when Spirit is calling back all of the children. Those children are us. We are all on the Earth at this time to find our purpose in regard to all the things that are happening, and will be happening. And we're here to find each other, to find people we can work with and help during this time of changes. The guides and spirits are here as support.

Learning how to put your gifts and your power to work in the most positive manner is what it's about right now. Many people are just existing, until one day they wake up and find out who they are. One day the time-lock in their brain releases. Right now, people use only about 10 percent of their brainpower, their ability. Once in a while we get into it a little deeper when we go into meditation or into our dream world. But the Creator thinks that most people are goofy enough with what they have already! Like the governor in a car, there's a time-lock on people's brains so they can't go beyond certain limits unless they are really, sincerely looking and trying. The Hopi say there was a time when the soft spot on the top of our head that we have as a baby remained open all during our lifetime. Through it, we were able to receive direct transmissions from the spirits. Then we got arrogant and *hardheaded* and Spirit sealed it over. So now if you want to get to the spirit powers, if you want to communicate, you've got to really reach out.

We are here on Earth because this is where people have all the possibilities for growing to their fullest potential. As you grow to another level of consciousness, you will be able to reach out and start helping other people. Then you will have begun the natural thinking that will take you to the Bright Day.

Chapter Eleven

Blueprint
To
The Year 2000

My predictions about the things that will occur during this time of Earth changes are based upon my dreams and visions. These have told me that there is nothing wrong with the Earth Mother that can't be cured by removing the goofy people who are creating the problems upon her. Consequently, I don't see as many major shifts as a lot of other people predict. There will be severe earthquakes and volcanic eruptions in some parts of the world. But I don't foresee a pole shift. I also don't see all the land masses upon the Earth being ripped apart. Why should the Earth suffer for problems created by humans?

What I do see overall is a lot of coastal flooding caused by the greenhouse effect; severe hurricanes and other storms that will affect many of the world's coasts, as well as inland areas; and increasing climatic changes. I do see some coastal areas being hit by large tidal waves that will completely submerge them. I see worldwide water shortages developing, and desertification affecting large parts of the globe.

I also see large-scale insect invasions caused by our overuse of pesticides that have wiped out the natural predators that feed on insects. I see many industrial accidents that will cause further pollution to the water, air, and soil in many parts of the world. I see more diseases over which people will have no control — diseases like AIDS.

All of this will contribute to the worldwide political and economic chaos that has already begun, causing many dinosaurs to die. Warfare that will result from the chaos will also aid this extinction process. But people who have changed their thoughts to natural ones, who have learned how to embrace the Earth Mother and all of her other children, will be in the right places at the right times, and will survive.

When things get really bad, I don't see most of the people in the large cities getting 20 miles beyond them. One of the problems in the cities will be the breakdown of services. In a major city, you are totally dependent on someone else for everything: electricity, natural gas, gasoline, public transportation, police, garbage collection, sewage systems, and most importantly, food and water. Keep in mind that all the food comes into the big city by truck or railroad. So if they stop running, you don't eat. Also remember that everyone who gives service to the city has to be paid.

The cities will become death traps. I feel you have to be at least 30 miles outside of any city to survive. You need to find a place that has a good water supply and natural fuel, like wood or coal. The area should also have other natural resources available.

I see people surviving in the remote areas all around the Earth. These will be people who know how to get out into the country or back into the deep recesses of the mountains, and how to survive there.

Don't pick a place down in a valley if there are big dams behind you. Earthquakes can cause major structural damage to dams in a matter of minutes. Coastal or lowland property will be in danger of flooding because of storms and tidal waves. With all the increasing pollution creating a warming trend, I feel there will be flooding much more quickly than most people realize.

Look at the political climate of any country you choose to survive in. There are many countries in the world that have very oppressive forms of government. Many of these give very few rights to their own people. In the case of national calamity and stress, these governments often turn on outsiders, especially if they happen to have a different color of skin or spiritual belief system. The countries that give the most freedom to their citizens are best to consider living in.

Now I'm going to give you my predictions for the changes I see on each of the major land masses upon the Earth Mother. They are listed in alphabetical order. The next chapter contains maps showing graphically the main points made here.

Africa

I foresee most of the African continent becoming more depleted of resources as the developed nations take what they need to survive. Because of this, I see mass starvation there. The Spirit has told me that up to 150 million people could perish in Africa due to starvation. I see the situation in Ethiopia, Chad, Zaire and the Sudan worsening. These countries, already being abandoned by the developed nations because there is no way they can continue to provide them with grain and food, will be the first to move toward starvation and major drought cycles. Other African countries will suffer later. Unless there are massive tree planting and regreening efforts, most of the African land — up to 80 percent — will become desert. I also see increased political unrest and economic chaos coming into many of the countries that are now primarily black-ruled. In white-ruled South Africa, I see more confrontations, with ensuing economic chaos. As a result, the conflict there will become ever sharper.

There is a major earthquake fault on the east coast of the continent, near what is called the Afar Triangle, which could produce a major quake that would separate off some of Africa.

I see jungles and oases being the safest areas to be, particularly oases in Nigeria and Algeria, and jungle land in Kenya, Zambia and Botswana. There will also be some safe spots along the southeastern coast of South Africa.

Asia

This is a big area with a lot of people living there, and I foresee a lot of Earth changes happening in Asia. This area of the Earth Mother will experience the whole gamut of Earth changes. To make them more understandable, I have divided Asia into several sections, depending mainly on similarities in the changes they can expect.

The Arabian Countries

A long time back I had a very powerful dream: Spirit showed me a map of Iran and the word "Iran" vanished off the map. I asked Spirit what was going to happen. Spirit said Iran would be completely destroyed by earthquakes, and by its neighbors. I feel Iran will continue to have conflicts with its neighbors and, eventually, the other Arabs are going to go in and use their finishing touches on them. Iranians are so completely warped in their thinking, they will die to the last one — at least all of them who are still in agreement with the late Mr. Khomeini. It will be very similar to what happened in Germany. Hitler was ready to scorch the Earth all over Europe, all the way back to his little fading castle. There is that same mentality in Iran.

Until that time, Iran will continue to have political oppression. It will also be hit by earthquakes. Lebanon will continue to have warfare, making its land unsafe. Libya will experience major economic problems. Iraq and Syria will have internal political problems, and these two countries will also have conflicts with each other, other Arab nations, and Israel. Iraq will be a major disruptive force in this area.

The people in Saudi Arabia and in the smaller, but rich, Arabian countries will have some comfort in their money for a time. But when there is no food to buy, all their money will be small comfort.

I see the possibility of a nuclear conflict in this area between 1994 and 1997. If this happens, it is likely that Israel will be involved in the havoc.

My greatest concern for all these countries is that water will become increasingly harder to get. But I see people surviving even here. All over the world, the people who live close to the land will survive.

India, Pakistan, and Bangladesh

In Pakistan and India, I see freak weather causing much destruction. There, great floods will hit in one area while there is drought in another. In India, more political unrest will disrupt the lives of people, causing more famine and mass starvation. There will also be insect invasions. But there will be some good spiritual leaders for India and Pakistan who will know what is happening and be able to guide people through the Earth changes. In Bangladesh, I see intense suffering from both storms and political unrest. There is a possibility of tidal waves submerging this country. I see more epidemic-type sicknesses striking India, Pakistan, and Bangladesh. India's biggest problem will be too many people and too few resources.

Southeast Asia
I foresee major food shortages here due in part to the continuing political struggles. Because of residues from warfare in this area, the food chain has been completely polluted. I expect to see blights on rice and other grains, and a shortage of potable water.

Indonesia, Malaysia, and the Philippines
While I do see a lot of people surviving on these islands, I also foresee them being affected by oceanic quakes, monster typhoons and climatic changes. There will also be starvation because of over-fishing and ocean pollution.

The more developed islands, particularly in the Philippines, will also experience political and economic chaos as their ties with the developed nations are forcibly severed.

Japan
For Japan I see many more earthquakes, some volcanic eruptions, and severe flooding. These, combined with industrial pollution and the damage that will follow earthquakes, will make the area a very difficult place in which to survive.

All of this will plunge Japan into economic chaos. Ultimately, I see Japan as a much smaller land area with very little evidence of its former development.

China

I see a great deal of hunger caused by crop failures and climatic changes with resulting political unrest. China will experience a lack of resources in many forms. For instance, there will be increasing fuel shortages because the Chinese have stripped the natural forests from much of the land; the people will have to search farther all the time just to get fuel to cook their food and otherwise provide for themselves.

I also foresee major earthquakes striking in different parts of this country.

Korea and Mongolia

The Mongolians will survive by roving as they have in many different periods of history — but only those who are wise enough to become nomadic again.

Korea, because of the warfare there, has depleted land and heavy water pollution. These conditions will result in major food shortages and severe economic problems.

Union of Soviet Socialist Republics

Russia will suffer from continuing ethnic unrest. The resulting political problems will cause further food shortages and famines, because people will not have the time to tend their crops. Russia will become more dependent on outside sources for food, until these sources fail. Part of the crop failure in Russia is a result of the Chernobyl nuclear disaster.

More major earthquakes will hit the country, as will extreme changes in weather. There will be increasing water shortages.

I do see an awakening in some parts of Russia to their old shamanic knowledge. This will eventually result in prophetic knowledge coming out of Russia to other parts of the planet.

Turkey

Turkey will experience a major drought that will force many of its people to become refugees.

Australia

In Australia there are some good areas away from the big cities, and lots of wildlife. But there are also a lot of very dry areas. Look for places with water. There will be climate changes and volcanic activity here.

There will also be earthquakes, tidal waves and extreme drought. I expect to see a lot of animal deaths — both wild and domestic — caused by pollution, particularly chemical pollution.

There will be many safe areas in Australia, particularly in the rain forests and in other areas that have water.

New Zealand

New Zealand is one of my favorite places in the world. It has a good climate, good government, and friendly people. There will be some volcanic activity and climate changes but there are many good, safe places here.

With the exception of the major urban areas, I see New Zealand as being safe. As folks get off into more isolated areas, they will form groups that will survive. People who know how to live off the land will have a good chance here. I see Australians and New Zealanders continuing in their way of life longer than people in many other parts of the world.

The Pacific Islands

Like the Philippines and Indonesia, the Pacific Islands will be affected by climatic changes, monster typhoons and oceanic quakes. They will also experience economic problems because they will be isolated from their former sources of revenue and will have to survive on their own self-reliance skills. There will also be some hunger because of over-fishing and other problems with the ocean waters. Yet, many people will survive.

Central And South America

In Central and South America, I see many areas that will experience an increase in the number of earthquakes and volcanic eruptions. Their effects will be worsened by major climatic changes. There will be droughts which will create more starvation than already exists.

Survival in Central and South America will be possible only away from the big cities. Mexico City, Lima, Buenos Aires and all the other large cities will become death traps here, too.

As less food is produced, life in these countries will become more chaotic. That means any foreigners in these countries will suffer. They will be totally regarded as people who don't fit in. Unless North Americans and Europeans can find isolated, safe retreats within Central and South America, there will be no place for them here.

I see the major volcanic and earthquake activity taking place in Guatemala, Mexico, Peru, Chile and Costa Rica. There will be major destruction of the cities in these countries, particularly Mexico City.

The continuing depletion of the rain forest will cause drought, then famine. There will be mass starvation throughout the area, and major epidemics, which will increase political and economic chaos.

There will be safe areas, and people will survive if they learn how to be with the land. I expect those Native people here who remember the natural world, to retreat from civilization and make it to the Bright Day.

The Atlantic Islands

Cuba, Haiti, the Dominican Republic, Puerto Rico and the other islands will experience coastal flooding, heavy storm damage with hurricane velocity winds, and a deepening poverty cycle. Still, people who know how to live with the land will survive here also.

196

Europe

In Europe there are many places opening up on the land. Those people who have enough sense to return to natural living will find these places throughout Europe. There are still many European people who love the land, and I see an increasing spiritual awareness in their relationship with the Earth. As people open up to loving the land and treating it in a sacred manner, their chances of survival will be greatly improved. We must remember that the reason for the Earth changes is because of the imbalances caused by the way humans have been treating the Earth.

In Europe I see the food situation becoming harder because of the amount of food that is imported. There are some areas that will have more food for longer periods of time. I see these particularly in Germany, but also in other countries where people have enough sense to get away from the major cities as those places get more chaotic. People who avoid food shortages and unemployment will be able to survive. I see the people who move out into isolated areas in France and other countries surviving in groups, if they learn to live in harmony with the Earth.

Iceland

Iceland is a relatively safe place, although I expect some volcanic disturbances, climatic changes and new air currents. The same is true of the Faeroe and Shetland Islands.

Scandinavia

I see many people surviving in Denmark, Sweden, Norway, and Finland *if* these countries don't expand their nuclear industries. There will be some coastal flooding, particularly in Norway and Denmark, but the Earth changes will be relatively light here. However, there is a possibility of some chemical disasters in the area. And, as I've mentioned, *if the nuclear industry expands in this part of the world*, I'd expect the changes to be more severe. Due to pollution, much of the fish supply has been lost. People here will also need to pray for good crops.

The British Isles

The British Isles will continue to be buffeted, intermittently, by high winds. I also expect coastal flooding and some tidal waves. As economic conditions worsen, there will be more political unrest.

England may suffer much more than other parts of the world simply because there is not enough food production in the country.

Sections of Scotland, Ireland and Wales, where people remember how to work with the land, will fare better than other parts of this area.

The Netherlands

The Netherlands will definitely suffer from severe flooding. It is possible that some parts of this country will be largely submerged during the changes. Many people will have to seek higher ground.

Germany

In Germany, many people are opening up very strongly to include the Earth Mother in their spiritual ways. This is good. People are also becoming more health food conscious. There are already a lot of gardens in Germany but some of the farmers could open up their farms and rent garden spots to people from the city. This would help provide food for more people during the changes. It would also teach people how to share and work together, and open up to the Earth spirit of the land. If you go to the power spots on the land and pray, the spirits will tell you how to live.

Although there is much that is good happening in Germany, it is not enough. Germany has to become more aware of industrial pollution. One major chemical or nuclear catastrophe could destroy much of the country, and I foresee the possibility of chemical or nuclear disasters throughout Germany. I also see worsening pollution, water shortages, and industrial accidents of various kinds.

My greatest concerns are for the big cities and for the areas near nuclear plants. If you can get away from both, it will increase your chances of survival. I see sicknesses coming to Germany over which people will have no control. This will be a result of both pollution and the weakening of people's immune systems.

Another concern I have for Germany is the rise in certain political beliefs that reflect the old Hitler regime. Governments that repress people will make survival a lot less likely.

There is a possibility of some volcanic activity in southern Germany. In East Germany, I see more Earth changes on account of its industry. However, there will still be some safe areas.

I see an awakening in some Germans who will bring a new spiritual awareness to Eastern Europe.

Poland, Czechoslovakia, Hungary, Romania and Bulgaria

All of these countries are heavily polluted, in part from their heavy dependence on diesel fuel with its bad effects on agriculture. The land is depleted. With the exception of Poland, these countries will be continuing toward famine. Poland, where the land is not so damaged, will be helping to feed other people as they restore their land.

Switzerland and Austria

Both of these countries will experience some major earthquake activity in their southern areas. They also have pollution problems, and could experience industrial accidents, food and water shortages, and changes of climate.

Italy and Yugoslavia

Both of these countries will have major earthquake activity. They also will have pollution, accidents, and water problems. Italy will see more volcanic activity.

Portugal, Spain, France, Luxembourg and Belgium

These areas will experience moderate to heavy drought and extreme climatic changes. Coastal areas will have flooding, high winds, and the possibility of tidal waves. These will bring about food shortages, and resultant political and economic unrest.

North America

Canada

I see much of Canada as being a good place to live. There is still a lot of open land, good fish and wildlife, and many other wild foods to harvest. Be aware that it does get cold there, and the further north you go, the colder it gets. It would be very hard to survive as a vegetarian in Canada. Except for the major cities, there are still a lot of good places. If you're in Alberta, be sure you have plenty of water as droughts are a real possibility throughout the Prairie Provinces.

I must say, in all fairness, that I feel much safer in Canadian cities than I do in most cities in the United States. But I feel all cities of major size have too many people competing for the same resources.

I also foresee the possibility of insect invasions in Canada, and of some climatic changes. Nonetheless, away from cities, this is a relatively safe area to be.

Greenland

This is another relatively safe area, although it will experience some volcanic eruptions.

The United States

In the United States, the areas to avoid are the big cities. They will continue to decline. I see things getting really bad in some of the big cities of the United States before they do in the cities of Europe. The AIDS epidemic in the major cities, along with new illnesses I foresee, may overload the health services to the point that there will be very little care available for all the sick people. This, of course, will be a real problem first in New York and San Francisco. I see, initially, the least livable cities being New York, Washington, D.C., Detroit, Philadelphia, and Miami. Other cities will follow.

I see that the northern United States and Canada, particularly away from the cities, will provide some safe areas. Some of the areas in the Southwest are going to experience major Earth changes. I foresee most of the Midwest eventually becoming a desert area. The major problem with the East Coast is that there are just too many people. If people want to survive there, they will have to move away from the populated areas. As the system breaks down in these cities, there will be major garbage pile-ups, and even more pollutants going into the water system.

I expect a number of earthquakes in the United States. One in California, from San Francisco south, will cause major destruction. There will be another in the Midwest along the New Madrid fault in the Mississippi River Valley, possibly creating a whole new lake; but definitely causing the Mississippi to change course. There will also be earthquakes in South Carolina, where Charleston is on a major earthquake fault, in North Carolina, in the New York City area, in Alaska, Montana, and Arkansas.

The Northeast Coast, at least from Boston to Washington, D.C., will be uninhabitable due to increasing pollution, an inability to dispose of waste, major epidemics in addition to AIDS, and seismic activity.

The entire East Coast will experience flooding and damage from severe hurricanes, which will increase in intensity.

Following is a state-by-state breakdown of some of the things I foresee happening.

ALABAMA — Some areas are all right, but there is the possibility of large storms and flooding along the Gulf Coast.

ALASKA — If you can handle the cold climate, there are many good areas. There is plenty of wildlife and fish. In many places, you can raise food. There will be earthquakes occurring and volcanoes erupting, so take these into account when selecting a location. Stay away from the cities.

ARIZONA — In northern Arizona, I prefer the Prescott and Flagstaff areas. Southern Arizona is too dry for survival, and Phoenix is a hell-hole.

ARKANSAS — This state is all right except for possible earthquakes. Stay away from cities and watch out for storms.

CALIFORNIA — There will be a major earthquake that will affect the coast of California from San Francisco south. I expect major destruction along the coast, and for a distance inland in the southern part of the state. The Sierra Nevada Mountain areas, north of Bishop and north of Sacramento, will be good places to be in this state. Stay away from all the large cities.

COLORADO — This state has many good areas. However, the Rocky Mountain Flats nuclear site has polluted the soil and water in an area near Denver. Be careful if you are looking at land there.

CONNECTICUT — This state has too many people in too small an area, plus a lot of industry. It will become uninhabitable along with the rest of the Northeast megalopolis.

DELAWARE — I feel Delaware has too many people and too much industry. It is also vulnerable to flooding and major hurricanes.

FLORIDA — I would not want to be on the east coast of Florida because of flooding, or in the south which will have increasing drought, then submersion by tidal wave. From Orlando to the Georgia border is safe, but watch out for water pollution.

GEORGIA — Stay away from the major cities. Watch out for flooding and storms on the coast.

HAWAII — Hawaii will experience climatic changes,

monster storms, and oceanic quakes; volcanoes will continue to erupt. There will be economic chaos as people are cut off from their former sources of revenue. However, Hawaii will still provide a lot of good areas in which to survive the changes.

IDAHO (north) — Northern Idaho is a good area. Consequently a lot of survivalists, including some very strange ones, have settled there. Be cautious about the humans.

IDAHO (south) — Because of the vast nuclear generating plants east of Boise, I'd avoid this area.

ILLINOIS — This state has some good areas. Stay away from Chicago and other cities. Check out any area for all possible forms of pollution.

INDIANA — There are still many good areas, if you avoid the industrial section, and thoroughly check for pollution.

IOWA — Iowa has some good places. But with such intensive farming, watch out for pesticides in the soil and water. It borders the drought belt and could become part of it.

KANSAS — Kansas will be suffering more severe drought. It also has a lot of chemicals in the soil and water because of current farming practices.

KENTUCKY — This state has many good areas if you stay away from the cities. Become a hill person; there are still places to live in the hills.

LOUISIANA — Some areas are all right, but there is the possibility of large storms and flooding.

MAINE — Most of Maine will be a good area for raising food and for general survival. Here I feel good even along the coast.

MARYLAND — Stay away from cities and watch out for storms. If you are in rural areas there is a chance for life.

MASSACHUSETTS — The western and central parts of the state are good, once you're out of the big city area.

Check for possible pollution of all kinds.

MICHIGAN — This state has many good areas. Stay away from Detroit. Watch for rising water levels on the Great Lakes.

MINNESOTA — This state has many good places. The northern area has cheap land. Be prepared for the cold.

MISSISSIPPI — Some areas are all right, but there is the possibility of large storms and flooding. The government there may become more repressive.

MISSOURI — There are many good areas. Lots of old people have lived on the land for years here. Check your water sources, and be careful about possible pollutants.

MONTANA (east) — This area is in a drought belt. It won't have sufficient water for growing anything.

MONTANA (west) — Western Montana is good, with lots of wild game. Remember there could be earthquake activity in the state.

NEBRASKA — Some areas may be safe, but be sure you have water. Nebraska borders the drought belt and could become part of it. It also has a lot of farm pollution.

NEVADA — Only northern Nevada presents the chance of survival, particularly in the mountainous parts. Southern Nevada, besides being dry, is the location of the federal government's nuclear bomb test site. Stay away.

NEW HAMPSHIRE — New Hampshire is a good place. Because of proximity to the Northeast megalopolis, watch for potential pollution.

NEW JERSEY — New Jersey is in the middle of the Northeast megalopolis that I expect to be uninhabitable. It is not good for survival.

NEW MEXICO — Go to the areas where there are mountains and trees. Be sure that you have water.

NEW YORK — The western and northern parts of the state are good. There are many wild plants and animals left in these areas. Watch for chemical and nuclear pollution.

NORTH CAROLINA — This is a state with lots of good places to raise food but try to learn to eat wild plants also.

Storms will continue to cause damage, seemingly randomly.

NORTH DAKOTA — This state is in a drought belt. It won't have sufficient water for growing anything.

OHIO — There are some good areas in the southwestern portion of Ohio. Keep away from the cities, and land polluted by farming.

OKLAHOMA — If you have water, this state is all right. This is a good area to use a windmill for pumping water; a side benefit of this could be electricity. Tornadoes and thunderstorms are likely to increase in intensity.

OREGON — Contains many good areas, but be sure of the water supply. There is toxicity in many areas.

PENNSYLVANIA — Pennsylvania is good from Scranton west. There are many good deer herds, other wildlife, and lots of wild plants. I could live well here. Check areas for possible sources of chemical or nuclear pollution.

RHODE ISLAND — I feel Rhode Island has too many people and too much industry. It is also vulnerable to flooding and major hurricanes.

SOUTH CAROLINA — This is a state with lots of good places to raise food but try to learn to eat wild plants also. Storms will continue to cause damage, seemingly randomly. Watch for flooding by the Atlantic in low-lying areas. Remember there is the possibility of earthquake activity here.

SOUTH DAKOTA — This state is in a drought belt. It won't have sufficient water for growing anything.

TENNESSEE — This is a state with lots of good places to raise food but try to learn to eat wild plants also. Storms will continue to cause damage, seemingly randomly.

TEXAS (east) — If you have water, this area is all right. Tornadoes and thunderstorms are likely to increase in intensity. This is a good area to use a windmill for pumping water and producing electricity. The coastal areas will have some tidal waves.

TEXAS (west) — This area is too dry for survival.

UTAH — This state is all right if you stay away from

the dry areas. Be very cautious where it borders Nevada because of the nuclear bomb test site located there.

VERMONT — This is a good state but be sure to check out potential pollutants in soil, air and water.

VIRGINIA — This is a state with lots of good places to raise food but try to learn to eat wild plants also. Storms will continue to cause damage, seemingly randomly. Watch for flooding by the Atlantic in low-lying areas.

WASHINGTON — Stay north of Seattle and east of the Cascades. I would not want to be in the Hanford nuclear reservation area, or the adjacent Tri-Cities. I think there is a good possibility that Tacoma will be wiped out when Mt. Rainier — the Grandfather — erupts. Be sure you have good water.

WEST VIRGINIA — This is a state with lots of good places to raise food but try to learn to eat wild plants also. Storms will continue to cause damage, seemingly randomly.

WISCONSIN — This state has many good areas. It can get cold.

WYOMING — There will be some good places in this state. Be sure you are in an area with a good supply of water. There could be some earthquake activity in the northern part of the state.

Chapter Twelve

Earth Changes Maps

On the following eleven pages are maps outlining the changes I discussed in the preceding chapter. The placement of a key symbol (below) on a map *does not* indicate the specific location of the Earth change predicted, but indicates it will happen within that country or area. Mild pollution or mild water shortages are not shown on the maps; I expect them to be occurring globally.

- ⟋🜨 — volcanic activity
- ⫸〰⫸ — possible earthquakes
- 🄳 — drought
- ▦ — area becoming desert
- ⟨☁⟩ — climatic changes
- 🦗 — insect invasions
- ⌒⌒⌒ — flooding
- ⟋(— possible tidal wave
- ☁⚡ — severe storms (hurricanes, tornadoes, etc.)
- 🄼 — moderately polluted areas
- 🅂 — severely polluted areas
- ☹ — possible industrial accidents (chemical or nuclear)
- 🌳 — possible nuclear conflict
- (💲) — economic chaos
- ⋉⊃ — animal deaths
- 🄵 — food shortages
- [F] — famine
- ★ — good amount of safe areas existing in the country
- 🏌 — political unrest
- ⚯ — epidemics

208

Africa

*(**Note:** Most of Continent Turning to Desert)*

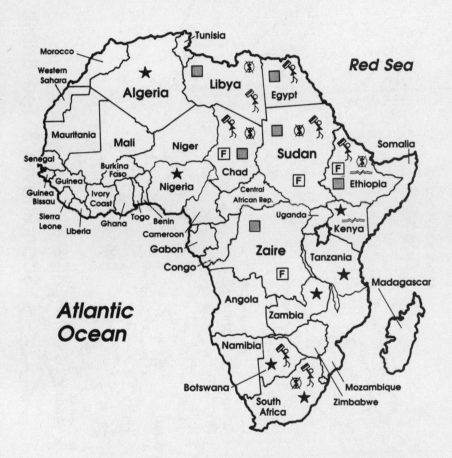

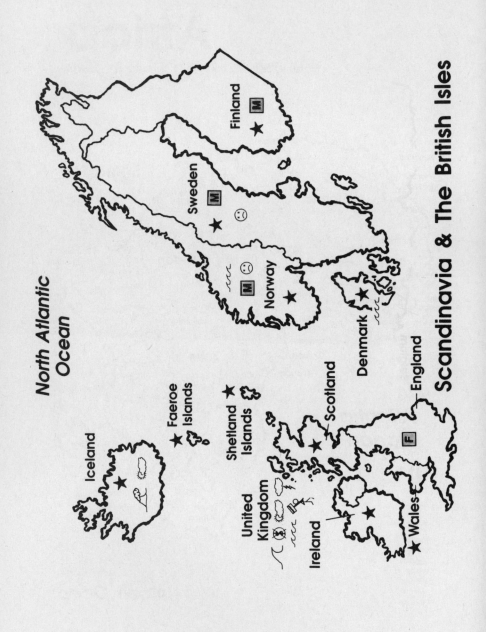

Scandinavia & The British Isles

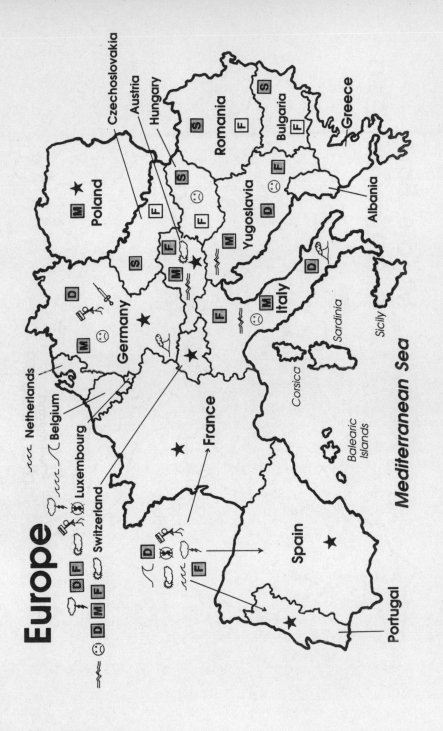

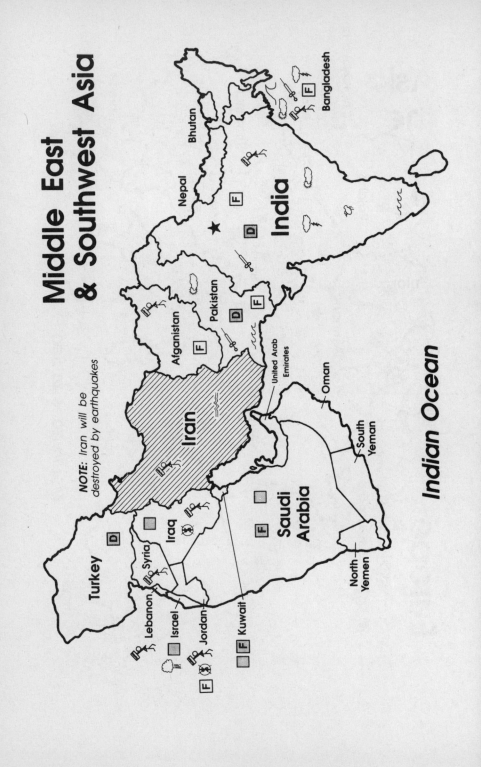

Middle East
& Southwest Asia

NOTE: Iran will be
destroyed by earthquakes

Indian Ocean

Asia & the USSR

Union of Soviet Socialist Republics

Mongolia

Japan

China

Korea

Taiwan

Philippines

Burma

Laos

Southeast Asia

Thailand

Vietnam

Indian Ocean

Kampuchea

Malaysia

Borneo

Sumatra

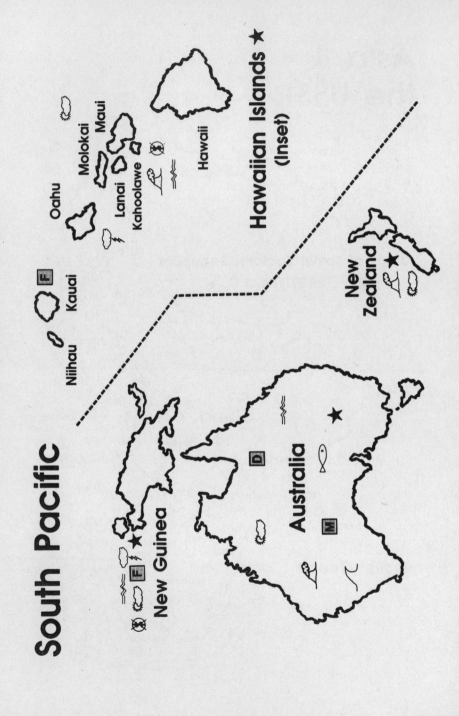

South Pacific

Niihau

Kauai

Oahu

Molokai

Maui

Lanai

Kahoolawe

Hawaii

Hawaiian Islands ★
(Inset)

New Guinea

Australia

New Zealand

Central & South America

Note: Central & South America will experience food shortages, political and economic chaos, epidemics, and drought.

Canada & Alaska 〰️ ★

Note: *Avoid circled areas.* ◉

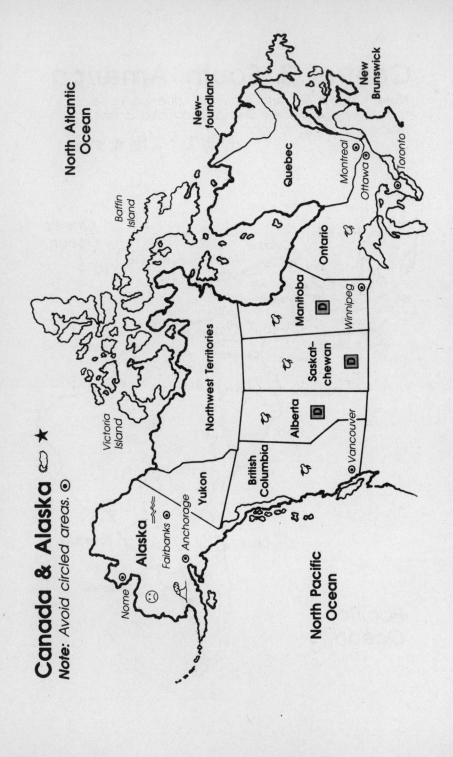

North Atlantic Ocean

New-foundland

New Brunswick

Quebec

Montreal ◉

Ottawa ◉

Toronto ◉

Baffin Island

Ontario

Manitoba

Winnipeg ◉

Northwest Territories

Saskat-chewan

Victoria Island

Alberta

Vancouver ◉

British Columbia

Yukon

Alaska

Fairbanks ◉

◉ Anchorage

Nome ◉

North Pacific Ocean

Western U.S.A.
Note: *avoid circled areas.* ⊙

Midwestern U.S.A.

Note: *avoid circled areas.* ⊙

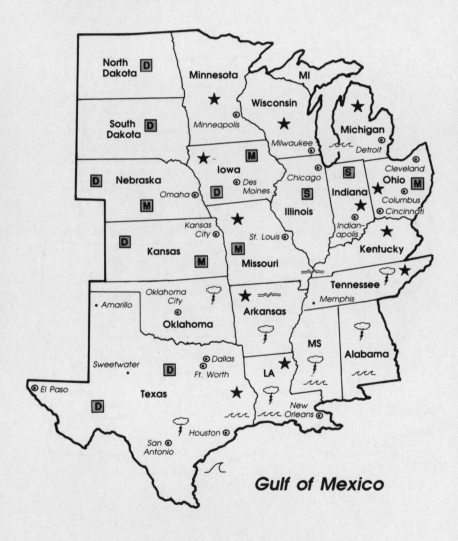

Chapter Thirteen

The New Earth

After all the territory we have covered in this book, you must understand by now why the Earth cleansing is necessary. Too many humans have become out of balance on the Earth Mother. Although all of creation once spoke the same language, humans, with their egos, became crazy and started to misuse and abuse the rest of creation. They soon forgot the language, and could no longer communicate.

After the cleansing, we will be relearning the language of nature. We will be learning to live upon the Earth without harming it. A great part of our work will be restoring balance in the rest of nature: reseeding the desert areas and those lands that have been clear-cut, helping endangered species to recover. We will be using permaculture for sustained yield without destroying the land, performing again the ceremonies to honor the Earth and the elements, and listening to the Creator's instructions for the renewal of the Earth.

Even now, many of us are trying to help nature to recover. Up on Vision Mountain, we have not allowed any hunting in all the years we have lived there. That is to allow the animal populations to recover. We have helped by feeding the deer in the winter when there is not enough food because of snow. We encourage birds to live with us by growing plants that give seed to them. We protect the snakes from being killed, never cut living trees for wood, and work for the survival of all creation in every way possible.

As part of the transformation, we are going to see some of the old traditions of the Native tribes coming back. In fact, some are already being practiced. The Bear Tribe, for example, is run by a council circle that allows everyone an equal voice in decisions. But even with this kind of process, decisions are ultimately made by Spirit. When Spirit tells us to act in a certain way, we listen. If Spirit were to tell us to move, for instance, we would move, since Spirit knows more about safe places than we do.

Also as part of the transformation, we will be learning important lessons about our over-dependence on technology. As I've said, I don't have anything against the light bulb, but technology has been over-used. When we reach the time when technological gadgets no longer work, you may find that you don't need a lot of things that you have now. Look at the example of my Maori brothers and sisters. They had a highly evolved civilization in some areas of the world. But when they got to New Zealand, they didn't need everything their civilization had developed, so they let go of the excess.

There are old dances for renewing the Earth. Humans will have time again to learn to dance them and to learn other sacred ways. We need to relearn that we are here to be happy and to dance upon the Earth. In healing the Earth, humans will also heal themselves, for there will be no more separation between the Earth Mother and her two-leggeds.

As human beings relearn their balance with nature, they will become healthier in body as well as spirit. When people are no longer in stress and out of balance, Spirit will let them live longer. It is said that the Incas of Peru used to live to be 350 years old. Many of my tribespeople lived to be 120, even 140, before the coming of the white man. This was particularly true of the medicine people who learned from the bears. Some of them would go into states of hibernation, sleeping through the winter and getting ready for life again in the spring. The aging process slows down when you are no longer at war with the Great Spirit. The Spirit becomes your total teacher. We have so much to relearn that it is good we'll have this help.

We are told that after the changes, we'll be learning how to rejuvenate our bodies. This will be easier because we will no longer have people around who are polluting the air, water and earth. We will have more real food and pure air and water. There will be fewer people competing for the natural resources. And all the little games of ego will have ended.

When you come into your full power as a human being, you don't have any fear anymore and you don't have any false challenges left in life. Then you can afford to be generous and loving to everybody, because you aren't afraid that somebody might take something away from you. You can even free yourself of the selfish possessiveness that people in society now try to pass off as love. This is because you will come to understand that you have enough love in yourself *for yourself*, and for others too. Those people close to you will be getting the juice, and you're getting the juice, and it's beautiful.

After the period of cleansing, we'll be going into the fifth world. The people moving into this world will be from all over the globe, but they will all share the same level of consciousness, found in their own individual ways.

I've had dreams in which I'm at a place, and a small group of people comes over a hill. We all embrace and say, "Brother, Sister, you survived." In this world, there aren't any "isms." We don't ask, "Well, what church do you belong to?" or "What this or that do you belong to?" None of that matters.

After the cleansing, we will see only people who know how to reach out and learn. We'll see people who are always seeking more spiritual knowledge. People will know that their survival during the Earth changes came about because they had made a good effort to live in love and harmony.

In the teachings of my people, there are eight degrees of power. The eighth degree is where you are on the same level as the spirits all of the time. You talk with them and think with them. During and after the cleansing, many of the great spirit teachers will take human form and walk among us.

Back in the 1880's when Wovoka, the Paiute Ghost Dance prophet, saw his vision, he spoke of what would happen after the Earth changes. He said, "When all the little dreams of Buffalo, Man and Horse are gone . . . we come together as one." When this happens, we will look again upon a beautiful and unspoiled land. It will be paradise restored. Ho! It is good!

Chapter Fourteen

The New Earth Workbook

Now that you've read about what is happening with the Earth, and what will happen in the future, it is time for you to do some things to rid yourself of whatever vestiges of dinosaur-thinking you have. This chapter will provide you with some starting places for doing that.

This part of the book is your workbook, your chance to plan your own methods of preparation for the changes, and of Earth healing. Rather than leave room for you to write in the book (which most people don't do anyway), I am asking that you get some recycled paper to put your ideas down on. Then put those pages in a recycled folder, envelope or notebook. Take this notebook out once a month and review your goals. See what you can do to meet ones you haven't. Celebrate those that you have.

Preparing For The Changes

1. My plans for learning to hear the Earth better include:
2. I will do the following things to learn more about the area in which I live and its potential for weather changes or seismic events:
   Activity   Date of Completion
3. Having learned about potential problems in my area, I will do the following to prepare:
   Activity   Date of Completion
4. I will do the following to help other people learn about these potential problems, and things they can do to prepare:
   Activity   Date of Completion
5. I will plan my car survival kit, and have it ready by:
   It will contain the following items:
6. I will have my five-day food survival kit ready by:
   It will contain the following items:
7. I will have a clear idea about where I would retreat if something happened in my city/area by:
8. I will have that place prepared by:
9. My water source will be:

10. My long-term food supply will be ready by:
    It will contain:
    It will be stored in the following types of containers:
11. My supply of clothing will be ready by:
    It will contain:
12. My medical storage will be ready by:
    It will contain:
13. My plans for networking with others during the changes are:

Healing The Earth Now

In the following exercises, as appropriate, include a date of completion after each item you plan.
1. I will make prayers to the keepers of my area in the following way(s):
2. I first thanked rain spirits on:
3. I will call weather people about speaking positively of rain and snow by:
4. I have these other ideas about relating to the weather:
5. I plan to landscape my area in the following ways, in keeping with the weather now:
6. I will keep my thermostat no higher than:
7. If I use it at all, I will keep my air conditioner no colder than:
8. I will keep my hot water heater no hotter than:
9. I will stop flushing my toilet so much by:
10. I will get a water filter by:
11. I will begin using graywater in the following ways:
12. I will do my 5-gallon bath experiment on:
    Here are my observations:
13. I will use these other methods to limit my water usage:
14. I will adopt the following body of water:
    These are my plans for taking care of it:
15. I will begin thanking the water spirits by:
16. I have the following ideas about water use and respect:

17. I will plant my first garden this year. I will prepare for this by:
18. I will expand my garden this year. I will prepare for this by:
19. I will learn how to compost by:
20. I will begin composting by:
21. I will learn about permaculture or other new gardening methods by:
22. I have these other ideas about gardening:
23. I will learn about taking care of live Christmas trees by:
24. I will do the following to help stop deforestation:
25. I will begin supporting Native peoples by:
26. I will find out about businesses that respect the Earth in the following ways:
27. I will start doing business with these companies or individuals by:
28. I am boycotting the following products for the following reasons:
29. I will find out how my lawmakers relate to the Earth and then:
30. I will write to my local newspapers about:
31. I will adopt the following road:
    I will do the following with it:
32. If I have a cat, I'll put a bell — being sure to use a break-away collar — on him or her by:
33. If I smoke for recreation, I will do the following to learn how to quit:
34. I will stop smoking by:
35. I will find out about biodegradable cleaners and start using them by:
36. I will stop using harsh chemicals and replace them with:
37. I will do the following so I can stop using styrofoam:
38. I will stop using any items containing CFC's by:
39. I will begin visualizing the ozone layer by:
40. I will switch to the following recycled paper products:
41. I will snip six-pack rings by:

42. Here is my personal recycling plan:
43. I will do the following to make sure my appliances are working well and are energy efficient:
44. I will have my air conditioners serviced by:
45. I will cut my energy usage in the following ways:
46. I will do the following to cut down on using my car:
47. I will do the following about air pollution problems:
48. I will do the following about nuclear problems:
49. I plan to do the following to help educate people about population:
50. Here are some other ways I can think of to help the Earth now:

Attitudes

1. Here is my personal plan for getting rid of my old conditioning:
2. Here is my concept of how the New Earth will be:
3. Here are my suggestions for changing myself in necessary ways to be an active participant in the New Earth:
4. Here are the ways I'm going to help others reach the Bright Day:

Any Suggestions?

If you come up with any suggestions that you think would help others to heal themselves and the Earth, please let me know about them. Send them to:

Sun Bear
Earth Changes Ideas
P.O. Box 9167
Spokane, WA 99209-9167

Together, may we enjoy the Bright Day!

BIBLIOGRAPHY

Adams, Catherine F. and Martha Richardson: "Nutritive Value of Foods," United States Department of Agriculture *Home and Garden Bulletin*, No. 72.

Associated Press: "Redoubt Kicking More Ash in Alaska," January 9, 1990.

Associated Press: "If it Glows in the Dark, Don't Eat It," January 9, 1990.

Associated Press: "Rare Plants Given Low Priority," August 21, 1989.

Associated Press: "Coca Growers Killing Amazon Rain Forests," August 13, 1989.

Associated Press: "Toxic Pollutant Numbers Startle EPA," April 13, 1989.

Associated Press: "Eruptions Predicted for Craters of the Moon," Feb. 21, 1989.

Baldwin, Guy: *The Permaculture Activist* (a quarterly publication from Davis, California).

Ballentine, Rudolph: *Diet & Nutrition.* Honesdale, Pennsylvania: The Himalayan International Institute.

Bear Tribe Publishing: *Wildfire Magazine* (a quarterly publication):
Vol. 3 No. 3, Fall 1988
Vol. 3 No. 4, Winter 1988
Vol. 4 No. 1, Spring 1989
Vol. 4 No. 2, Summer 1989
Vol. 4 No. 3, Fall 1989
Vol. 4 No. 4, Winter 1989
Vol. 5 No. 1, Spring 1990

Booth, William: "Lake Victoria's Ecosystem, Vital to Millions, May be Unraveling," *The Washington Post*, June 5, 1989.

Bryant, Page: *The Earth Changes Survival Handbook.* Santa Fe, New Mexico: Sun Publishing Co.

Bryant, Page: *Earth Changes Now.* Santa Fe, New Mexico: Sun Books, 1989.

Brown, Tom, Jr.: *Tom Brown's Field Guide to Wild Edible and Medicinal Plants*. New York: The Berkley Publishing Group, 1984.

Brown, Tom, Jr.: *Tom Brown's Field Guide to Wilderness Survival*. New York: The Berkley Publishing Group, 1984.

Brown, Tom, Jr.: *Tom Brown's Field Guide to City and Suburban Survival*. New York: The Berkley Publishing Group, 1988.

Boston Globe: "British Experts Report Last Year Was Warmest on Record For the Earth," *San Diego Union*, February 4, 1989.

Buchman Ewald, Ellen: *Recipes for a Small Planet*. New York: Ballantine Books.

Campbell, Stu: *Let it Rot*. Pownal, Vermont: Storey Communications, Inc.

Colbin, Anne Marie: *The Book of Whole Meals*. New York: Ballantine Books.

Denver Post: "25 Percent of Species May Need Protection," *Denver Post*, August 19, 1989.

Der Speigel: "Tropical Forests: An Endangered Species," *World Press Review*, May 1989.

Donelan, Peter: *Growing to Seed*. Willits, California: Ecology Action.

Editor of Eagles Network News: *Eagles Network News*, (Salmon Arm, British Columbia, Canada), April, 1989.

Egan, Timmothy: "America's National Forests Are Falling Beneath the Saw," *New York Times News Service*.

Earth Works Group: *50 Simple Things You Can Do To Save The Earth*. Berkeley, California: Earthworks Press, 1989.

Elliot, Ann: *Fat Years, Lean Years*. Creative Living Center, California: Et Al.

Ephron, Larry: *The End: The Imminent Ice Age and How We Can Stop It*. Berkeley, California: The Institute for a Future.

Ferguson, Tom: *Medical Self Care*. California: Medical Self Care.

Ford, Frank with Jamie Buckingham: *The Coming Food Crisis*. Hereford, Texas: Chosen Books.

Fukuoka, Masanobu: *One Straw Revolution*. New York: Bantam Books.

Global Awareness in Action: "The Planetary Ecological Clock," *Global Awareness in Action*, (Anse St. Jean, Quebec, Canada).

Global Awareness in Action: "Some Facts About the Environment," *Global Awareness in Action*, (Anse St. Jean, Quebec, Canada).

Hamaker, John D.: *The Survival of Civilization*. Burlingame, California: Hamaker-Weaver Publishers.

Haycak, Cara: "Brazil: Global Stand-off," *Santa Monica News*, March 31, 1989.

Hemenway, Dan: *The International Permaculture Species Yearbook* (TIPSY). Maloy, Iowa: Yankee Permaculture.

Hertzberg, Vaughn, and Greene: *Putting Food By*. Lexington, Massachusetts: The Stephen Greene Press.

Houghton, Richard A. and George M. Woodwell: "Global Climatic Change," *Scientific American*, April, 1989.

Jeavons, John: *How to Grow More Vegetables*. Berkeley, California: Ten Speed Press.

Jochmans, J.R.: *Rolling Thunder: The Coming Earth Changes*. Albuquerque, New Mexico: Sun Publishing Co, 1981.

Johnston, Robert, Jr.: *Growing Garden Seeds*. Albion, Maine: Johnny's Selected Seeds.

Katzen, Mollie: *The Moosewood Cookbook*. Berkeley, California: Ten Speed Press.

Keys, Ken, Jr.: *The Hundredth Monkey*. Coos Bay, Oregon: Vision Books, 1982.

Kourik, Robert: *Designing and Maintaining Your Edible Landscape Naturally*. Santa Rosa, California: Metamorphic Press.

League of Women Voters Education Fund: *The Nuclear Waste Primer*. New York: Nick Lyons Books, 1985.

Los Angeles Times: "Dikes For California?" *Los Angeles Times*, August 20, 1989.

Loveday, Evelyn V.: *Home Storage of Vegetables and Fruits.*
Charlotte, Vermont: Garden Way Publishing.

Mead, Mark: "Surviving the 1990s," *Macrobiotics Today,*
February, 1989.

Mollison, Bill: *An Introduction to Permaculture.* Orange,
Massachusetts: Yankee Permaculture.

Mollison, Bill: *Permaculture: A Designer's Manual.* Tyalgum,
NWS, Australia: Tagari Publications.

Morris, Julie: "Wildfires to be Fought Hard," *USA Today,*
March 15, 1989.

Moskal, Jerry: "Pollution Worse, Lake Study Says," *USA
Today,* March 15, 1989.

Newman, Steve: "Earthweek: A Diary of a Planet" (syndi-
cated feature), *Spokesman Review:*
— Feb. 17, 1989
— Feb. 24, 1989
— Mar. 3, 1989
— Mar. 11, 1989
— Mar. 17, 1989
— Apr. 21, 1989
— May 19, 1989
— Jun. 2, 1989
— Jun. 16, 1989
— Jun. 23, 1989
— Jul. 7, 1989
— Jul. 21, 1989
— Jul. 28, 1989
— Aug. 11, 1989
— Aug. 25, 1989
— Nov. 10, 1989
— Dec. 8, 1989
— Dec. 15, 1989
— Dec. 29, 1989

Newsweek Magazine, Editors of: "Anatomy of an Oil Spill,"
Newsweek, September 18, 1989.

New York Times: "Good News for Elephants," *New York
Times,* June 12, 1989.

New York Times: "Blue Whale Closer to Extinction Than Thought," *New York Times*, June 20, 1989.

Oregonian, The, Editors of: "Forests: Management Practices Rapped as Crisis Looms," *The Oregonian*, October 30, 1989.

Pierce, Neal: "Trees and Cities: End Arborcide, Fight the Greenhouse Effect," *The Denver Post*, June 1, 1989.

Peterson, Bill: "Midwest Drought Is Older But Not Wider This Year," *Washington Post*, May 21, 1989.

Pilarski, Michael: *Friends of the Trees 1988 International Green Front Report*. Chelan, Washington.

Pontious, Robert V. and Anne M.: *Store, Stock Up, and Survive!* Self-published, 1980.

Ritter, Malcolm: "Ozone Hole May Increase the Risk of Skin Cancer in Southern Hemisphere," *Seattle Post Intelligencer*, July 27, 1989.

Research Report of the Orgone Biophysical Research Lab: *Pulse of the Planet* (a bi-annual publication). El Cerrito, California: Orgone Biophysical Research Lab.
Vol. 1 No. 1, Spring 1989.
Vol. 1 No. 2, Fall 1989.

Robbins, William: "Rain Helps New Corn; It's Too Late For Cattle," *The New York Times*, June 12, 1989.

Robertson, Laurel, Carol Flinders and Brian Ruppenthal: *The Deaf Smith Country Cookbook: Natural Foods for Family Kitchen*. Berkeley, California: Ten Speed Press.

Rogers, Marc: *Growing and Saving Vegetable Seeds*. Charlotte, Vermont: Garden Way Publishing.

Sehnert, Keith: *How To Be Your Own Doctor, Sometimes*. New York: Grosset and Dunlap.

Sidey, Hugh: "The Real Deficit is Water," *New York Times*, February 27, 1989.

Spokesman Review, the Editors of: "Part of Amazon Rain Forest Burned Down Last Year," *Spokesman Review*, June 15, 1989.

Stoner Hupping, Carol: *Stocking Up*. Emmaus, Pennsylvania: Rodale Press.

Sun Bear: *Buffalo Hearts*. Spokane, Washington: Bear Tribe Publishing, 1976.

Sun Bear: *At Home in the Wilderness*. Happy Camp, California: Naturegraph Publishers, 1968.

Sun Bear, Crysalis Mulligan, Peter Nufer, and Wabun: *Walk In Balance*. New York: Prentice Hall, 1989.

Sun Bear, Wabun, and Barry Weinstock: *Sun Bear: The Path of Power*. New York: Prentice Hall, 1987.

Sun Bear and Wabun: *The Medicine Wheel: Earth Astrology*. New York: Prentice Hall, 1980.

Sun Bear and Wabun with Nimimosha: *The Bear Tribe's Self Reliance Book*. New York: Prentice Hall, 1988.

Time Magazine, Editors of: "Endangered Earth Issue," *Time Magazine*, January 2, 1989.

Tye, Larry: "Global Warming Could Cause Power Shortages," *Spokesman Review*, May 17, 1989.

Washington Post: "Antarctica 'Hole' Increases Radiation Over Australia, New Zealand," *The Seattle Times*, July 27, 1989.

Werner, David: *Where There is No Doctor*. Palo Alto, California: Hesperian Foundation.

Whealy, Kent: *Seed Savers Exchange*. Decorah, Iowa.

Wicker, Tom: "The Great Forests Are Still Vanishing; We Must Plant More, Cut Less," *New York Times*, January 7, 1989.

Wiley, John P. Jr.: "Phenomena, Comment and Notes," *Smithsonian Magazine*, September, 1988.

Willey, Steve and Elizabeth: *Backwoods Solar Electric Systems 1989 Planning Guide*. Sandpoint, Idaho.

Wind, Wabun: *Woman of the Dawn*. New York: Prentice Hall, 1989.

Wind, Wabun and Anderson Reed: *Lightseeds*. New York: Prentice Hall, 1988.

Windishar, Anne: "It's a Big Year for Pine Butterflies," *Spokesman Review*, July 27, 1989.

About The Authors

Sun Bear is a Chippewa medicine man who founded the Bear Tribe, located near Spokane, Washington, which welcomes Indians and non-Indians as students, associates and members. The publisher of the magazine *Wildfire*, he is also a lecturer, teacher, and author of the books, *Sun Bear: The Path Of Power*, *Walk in Balance*, *At Home in the Wilderness*, *The Medicine Wheel*, *Buffalo Hearts*, and *The Bear Tribe's Self-Reliance Book*.

Wabun Wind, his medicine helper, holds an M.S. from the Columbia School of Journalism and has written articles for such magazines as *Life*, *McCalls*, and *New York*. She is the author of the books, *The People's Lawyers*, *Woman of the Dawn*, and *Lightseeds* (with Anderson Reed) and has worked with Sun Bear as co-author on a variety of books and publications. She is the founder of Wind Communications, a literary agency. She is also a transpersonal practitioner and ceremonial designer.

OTHER BOOKS FROM THE AUTHORS

The Path Of Power, by Sun Bear, continues to interpret ancient philosophies for today's readers. In *The Path Of Power*, readers will learn:

How to seek and find vision in their lives.

How to find and follow their own path of power.

Why their path of power is the reason for their being alive on the planet at this time.

Over 100,000 copies sold. Now in its third printing from Prentice Hall.

The Bear Tribe's Self–Reliance Book, by Sun Bear, Wabun, Nimimosha and the Tribe. New & Revised. A guide for everyone interested in returning to the land. It contains basic skills for re–establishing a proper relationship with the land and all beings upon it, as well as Native American and New Age philosophies, prophecies and visions.

The Medicine Wheel: Earth Astrology, by Sun Bear and Wabun. A system of Earth astrology to help guide people not only in their daily lives, but in their life path as well. The book combines Native legends, lore and wisdom, with the vision of Sun Bear to help the reader walk in balance on the Earth Mother.

Over 500,000 copies sold worldwide.

Woman Of The Dawn, by Wabun Wind. An unprecedented, behind–the–scenes look into the early days of the Bear Tribe, and a very human portrait of Sun Bear. Wabun retraces her steps along the path of inner discovery from successful New York writer to medicine helper to Sun Bear.

Lightseeds, by Wabun Wind and Anderson Reed. One of the most comprehensive books on crystals now available. With techniques ranging from the basic to the advanced, this book appeals to the novice enthusiast as well as the experienced practitioner.

Walk in Balance

The Path to Healthy, Happy, Harmonious Living

by Sun Bear with Crysalis Mulligan, Peter Nufer and Wabun

A personal survival manual that will help you live in balance with yourself, *Walk in Balance* contains Sun Bear's philosophy of healing and happiness along with tools for creating a vital, invigorating, low–stress life.

Walk in Balance offers a holistic pathway to personal enrichment and health.

Vision Quest

We have today to learn to get back into accord with the wisdom of nature and realize again our brotherhood with the animals and with the water and the sea.... The idea is trans-theological, it is of an undefinable, inconceivable mystery thought of as a power, that is the source and end and supporting ground of all life and being.

Joseph Campbell — *The Power of Myth*

The Vision Quest is a trans–cultural rite of passage, and a traditional ceremony among many Native tribes of this continent. The Bear Tribe has guided hundreds of people through the fasting-quest experience. The program begins with Earth awareness exercises and instruction to acquaint you with the vision quest process and to open your eyes, ears and heart to Mother Earth. After the instructional time, you are placed on the land and remain there fasting, seeking, crying for vision, for up to four days and nights. When you return from the quest, trained instructors are available to talk with you about your personal experience. Group sharing and ceremonies complement the individual quest and bring the program to a close.

We all have a powerful ally and helper in the natural world, there for the asking, especially so in the times of important life passages. For the past 15 years the Bear Tribe has offered a vision quest specifically designed for people in today's society. We invite you to join us.

Only by quieting yourself and searching within will you find your vision and your Path of Power — **Sun Bear**

For more information about the Vision Quest program, and current dates and locations, write:

Programs Office
PO Box 9167
Spokane, WA 99209

The Bear Tribe Introductory Program

"I stood on a hilltop and I was in total darkness. Everything seemed bleak and desolate until I prayed to the Creator. My hand was moved upward then. I pointed out into the darkness and a brilliant light came on. . . . Again and again, as I pointed my finger, lights glimmered out at me from the darkness. . . . The Great Spirit told me that the lights represented people who would come to me to learn, and then go back out into the world to use their new medicine knowledge." — **Sun Bear**

Our Apprenticeship Program is one for contemporary times, for the challenges of today. It begins with an intense 10–day introductory course. Students spend their time living and learning in a natural setting to experience the Earth as a teacher and healer. Sun Bear and Bear Tribe teachers offer a healthy mix of self–reliance, personal growth, ceremony, and the philosophies and traditions of Native American and other traditional, Earth–respecting peoples. The program is designed to introduce you to the sacred path and begin the foundations for you to make it your own.

What we teach is not abstract but very real, practical spiritual skills people can use and share.

What we are looking for are responsible people willing to act on this knowledge in their own lives, and then reach out to help others.

These people become apprentices of Sun Bear's vision.

For more information about the Bear Tribe's Introductory Program write:

Programs Office
PO Box 9167
Spokane, WA 99209

Bear Tribe Programs

Self–Reliance Intensive

This program was developed as a result of Sun Bear's concern that people be better prepared to live self–sufficiently during the coming Earth changes. We identify, harvest and store various foods, using solar drying, root cellaring, canning and freezing. Seed saving and storage are also taught. Basic Permaculture principles and techniques, leatherwork, shelters, tracking and stalking, hunting, weapon and tool care, emergency survival and first aid, medicinal plants, preparing salves and tinctures are some of the other topics covered.

Medicine Wheel Gatherings

Medicine Wheels made of stones, constructed by the original Native peoples, once spread all across this land. The wheel was a place for the people to share their teachings and conduct ceremonies. Sun Bear had a vision several years ago that told him *now* is the time for Medicine Wheels to return to this land as places of healing, sharing and teaching for Native and non–Native alike. A Medicine Wheel Gathering is a three–day symposium of great teachers from many different walks of life; a time to learn, share, nurture, celebrate, and feel your connection to the Earth.

Medicine Wheel Gatherings are held throughout the summer and fall at various sites across the USA.

for more information write:
The Bear Tribe • PO Box 9167 • Spokane, WA 99209